PRAISE FOR
ROCK RETIREMENT

"Too many books think retirement is just about finances. Instead, retirement is about looking at life in full and working out what it is you want to do and then turning to finances to make it happen. That's exactly the focus of this practical and helpful guide by Roger Whitney that will help you Rock Retirement."

—Andrew Scott,
Professor of Economics at London Business School and
Coauthor of *The 100-Year Life*

"Roger Whitney lays out a plan for today's modern retiree. If you are exhausted with being fed that retirement is the end game of life, then Roger's book is a must-read!"

—Darryl W. Lyons, Cofounder of PAX Financial
Group and Author of *Small Business Big Pressure: A Faith-based
Approach to Guide the Ambitious Entrepreneur*

"We live in a culture obsessed with 'retirement,' that magical time when we can leave work behind and do what we really want to do. And yet I observe time and time again that people focus only on what they're moving from—with little thought for what they're moving to. *Rock Retirement* is a guide for planning that rich season of life, based not just on money, but also on how to create meaningful relationships, memories, and legacy."

—Dan Miller, Author of *48 Days to the Work You Love*

"If you have ever thought of retirement and financial planning, *Rock Retirement* will show you how to create your own personal retirement masterpiece. Roger captures the 'art' of planning and framing your plan in a masterful way!"

—Reagan Lee Wagner, CEO, President, and Managing Principal of NFA Wealth Management

"Roger Whitney has the unique gift of taking a conversation that would typically be chock-full of numbers and calculations and transforming it into a deep discussion about your life and your vision of the future. His confidence in the retirement realm is the result of going on a journey with each and every investor he works with."

—Blaine Douglas, CIMA®, Managing Partner of Old Course Investment Partners, LLC

"Roger is the master! If you want to learn from the best on how to create an extraordinary retirement, one that will likely exceed your wildest imagination, this book is a must-read! I have seen nothing else like it."

—Robert Mallon, Cofounder, Rusty Lion Academy
(rustylionacademy.com)

"The mathematics of retirement is relatively simple. But figuring out how to actually enjoy your retirement is anything but. Roger Whitney does an excellent job helping prospective retirees to go beyond the 'simple math' and figure out what a meaningful retirement really means!"

—Michael Kitces, CFP®, Publisher of *Nerd's Eye View*
at kitces.com

"Roger Whitney is not just a great businessman and thought leader; he is genuinely interested in the people around him. He yearns for them to succeed—whatever that means to each person—and will do whatever he can to help them get there. This book represents the essence of his urgency to see people thrive."

—John Knowlton, CFP®, Cofounder of Oak Point
Financial Group

"When I sold my business, I worked with some of the best financial advisors as I prepared for retirement. My only regret is not being exposed to the concepts in *Rock Retirement* earlier. Roger's insights into the journey toward creating not just a great retirement but a great life are light years ahead of anything I've read."

—Bill Watkins, Cofounder of Rusty Lion Academy

"Roger Whitney takes a unique look at retirement. He looks beyond the finances required, to what it will take to Rock Retirement. I love his concept of making the most of the only life you have."

—Marc Miller,
Founder of Career Pivot (careerpivot.com)

"This is not your parents' retirement-planning book. Unlike traditional financial advisors, Roger Whitney understands that retirement planning is really about your life, not just your finances. Focusing just on the money side of retirement planning leads to a paint-by-numbers retirement that doesn't fit modern lives and won't fit you. In *Rock Retirement,* Whitney will help you to figure out what you want your life to look like, now and in the future, and he walks you through the steps you need to take to align your plans with your life."

—Emily Guy Birken,
Author of *The Five Years Before You Retire*

"If you're dreaming of a retirement free of worry, chaos and confusion, *Rock Retirement* will give you the clarity, a solid plan and fresh inspiration to help you get where you want to go."

—Jevonnah "Lady J" Ellison, Author of *Love Letters for Leading Ladies* and Founder of Maximum Potential Academy

A Simple Guide to Help You Take Control
and Be More Optimistic About the Future

ROGER WHITNEY CFP® CIMA® CPWA® AIF®

NEW YORK

NASHVILLE • MELBOURNE • VANCOUVER

ROCK RETIREMENT

Published in New York, New York, by Morgan James Publishing. Morgan James is a trademark of Morgan James, LLC. www.MorganJamesPublishing.com

The Morgan James Speakers Group can bring authors to your live event. For more information or to book an event visit The Morgan James Speakers Group at www.TheMorganJamesSpeakersGroup.com.

ISBN 978-1-68350-573-0 paperback
ISBN 978-1-68350-574-7 eBook
Library of Congress Control Number: 2017907110

Cover, Interior Design, and Illustrations by:
Megan Whitney
Creative Ninja Designs
megan@creativeninjadesigns.com

In an effort to support local communities, raise awareness and funds, Morgan James Publishing donates a percentage of all book sales for the life of each book to Habitat for Humanity Peninsula and Greater Williamsburg.

Get involved today! Visit
www.MorganJamesBuilds.com

CONTENTS

FOR MY MOM

ACKNOWLEDGMENTS

Thank you, Lord, for teaching me to trust in You.

Thank you to my wife, Shauna, for not giving up on me and always backing my crazy dreams. Thank you to my son, Spencer ("LK"). Your caring spirit and willingness to have deep conversations make me stronger. Thank you to my daughter, Emma. Your trailblazing spirit inspires me. So proud of you guys.

I love my family and the encouragement they have given me. Thanks Dave, Linda, Kevin, and Shelly, for adopting me. Thank you to my sisters, Joanne and Barbara. Thank you to my Aunt Patti and Uncle Tim for their constant encouragement and spirit.

I love my WWK family. Lorna and Phil, you're amazing partners. Thank you for always giving me space to explore (and for putting up with me!!). Dina, Brandy, Derek, Marc, Sean, Van, and Philip, I learn so much from you. Thank you.

Special thank you to Nichole ("Rock Star") Mills for the countless hours spent fine-tuning this book and the business. You are the gutter-bumpers that keep me on track and make it all happen. I couldn't have asked for a better teammate.

Thank you to my buddy Bob Bancroft for providing the spark. To my 48 Days Mastermind group for showing me how to live bigger. To my Rusty Lions, Bill Watkins and Robert Mallon for coaching me up.

Thank you to the TSG study group for showing me what real businessmen look like. Darryl Lyons, John Knowlton, Reagan Wagner, and Blaine Douglas, you guys are ballers.

Thank you to all whose counsel, encouragement, and butt-kicking influenced the creation of this book: Jamie Slingerland, Nick Pavlidis, Dan Miller, Joanne Miller, Big Bad Andy Traub, David (write a book) Hancock, Joe "Stacking Benjamins" Saul-Sehy, and Kevin Anderson.

Thank you to my writing partner, Emily Chase Smith. You made it happen.

Big Texas hugs to Morgan James Publishing (especially David Hancock and Megan Malone), proofreader Avery Auer, and illustrator Megan Whitney for cleaning up my literary mess and making me look good.

BIG THANK YOU to my clients and the *Retirement Answer Man* community. Your questions, corrections, feedback, enthusiasm, and encouragement fuel me. You are rocking life, and I'm honored to be a small part of your journey.

THE ALL-IMPORTANT DISCLAIMER

It's simple. Don't take advice from me. Well, at least not in this book or on my podcast. I know nothing about you, and you don't know much about me. It would be silly to give you advice. I only give advice to clients. I am a practicing financial planner and walk life with clients every day, helping them plan for, transition into, and live life in retirement. I serve them as a fiduciary. This means I understand their dreams, financial resources, and overall situation enough to give them advice. So consider this book as a source of helpful hints and education.

—Roger Whitney, CFP®, CIMA®, CPWA®, AIF®

P.S. My attorney says:

"Please remember that different types of investments involve varying degrees of risk, and it should not be assumed that future performance of any specific investment or investment strategy (including the investments and/or investment strategies referenced in this book) will be profitable, equal any corresponding indicated historical performance level(s), or prove successful. Due to various factors, including changing market conditions and/or applicable laws, the content may no longer be reflective of current opinions or positions. No reader should assume that any portion of this book's content serves as a substitute for personalized advice from the investment professional of his/her choosing.

"Opinions voiced in this book are for general information only and are not intended to provide specific advice or recommendations to any individual. All performances referenced are historical and no guarantee of future results. All indexes are unmanaged and may not be invested into directly."

P.P.S. Names, places, circumstances, and facts have been changed to protect the privacy of individuals.

NOTES FROM
THE AUTHOR

It's easy to get caught up in numbers. Numbers and the math used to manipulate them have an elegance to them. They're clean. Everything adds up nice and tidily. We financial planning folks tend to love math. It makes our job of advising you easy. We extract the numbers from your life, input them into our retirement calculator and use the result it spits out to tell you what you should do. Don't like the answer? "Sorry," we say. "The math doesn't lie."

If you listen to lazy retirement advice that can't see the human beyond the calculator, you may miss your life. I'm not exaggerating. You quite possibly could miss much of your glorious life trying to fit into the mathematical equation of retirement planning.

Your life is not a simple math problem to be solved. Your life is a big, hot, beautifully messy mix of needs, wants, desires, worries, relationships, struggles, achievements, setbacks, wins, losses, surprises, joys, sorrows, excitements, slumps, beginnings, endings and so much more. To really rock retirement, you'll need an agile approach that responds quickly to changes in your life and gives you the tools to make smart decisions.

It is my hope for you that you embrace all your power to intentionally build an amazing life and retirement…regardless of markets, economies or politics.

In this book, I show you how to move beyond rigid, simple math solutions so you can make the most of the only life you have.

Be well friend, and please Rock Retirement.

FOREWORD

I tell friends that I come from the Roger Whitney School of Financial Planning. What does that mean? It means that numbers are secondary to the art of planning a retirement.

Don't get me wrong. Both Roger and I have a deep respect for the "math" of retirement planning. Over the years I've seen Roger pore over spreadsheets and legal documents, mining them for information on how to get from here—the working days of now—to the elusive there of a realistic retirement date. He's great at it.

But, in what will be surprising to many readers, Roger explains in this book how traditional retirement planning methods used in the past don't really work any longer. Because "retirement" no longer means thirty years with the same company and a nice hefty pension, it's high time we all looked for more innovative planning.

Rock Retirement elevates the process of retirement planning from a simple math problem to a beautiful and life-fulfilling art form. Roger shows you how to discover your genuine dream, the one that has lived silently within you. If you're having trouble envisioning your own plan, don't worry. He even offers examples of how others have succeeded in making their own deep-seated dreams come true.

And the best part? This is a practical book filled with sensible ideas. So sensible you wonder why no one has offered this type of planning before now.

I love this book you're holding because the sheer creativity of Roger's suggestions is something we can all get excited about. That's saying something if you consider we're not talking about paintings or sculptures, but retirement planning. Suddenly this whole process has flipped from a dull "must do it" burden, to a cohesive, personal, wish-fulfilling process.

Congratulations on opening this mind-bending read. It's the gateway to focusing your time, energy, and money on a happier and more rewarding retirement.

—**Joe Saul-Sehy**
Creator of the Award-Winning *Stacking Benjamins* Podcast
(stackingbenjamins.com)

INTRODUCTION

Rock
Intransitive Verb
Slang: To be great, exciting, or fun

J im and Sally have been saving for retirement for years and feel ready for it. The nest has emptied, so the couple sits down with a financial advisor to cement their retirement plans.

When their advisor hits "calculate," the air leaves the room. The lifestyle they want during retirement remains out of reach without sacrifices. The magic number—the amount they need to live well—is eye-bulgingly big.

The advisor offers "solutions," but they all seem terrible: Work longer, live on less to save more, take more investment risks, or settle for less.

The couple shares a look that says, "We followed the game plan, so how did we get here?"

When Jim and Sally leave the conference room, they feel defeated.

The pair married in their early twenties and, like most young couples, spent more than they should have early on. They ate out a lot, drove nice cars, and bought a bit too much house. When they were twenty-eight and their first child arrived, they knew they needed to get their financial act together. They paid off their credit cards and met with a financial planner to prepare for college costs and retirement.

This planner recommended that they contribute to their 401(k) and set up a 529 college savings plan for their daughter. He explained that if they contributed $1,000 per month to their 401(k) account, by age sixty they could be millionaires (almost $2.8 million with a return of ten percent). The key, the planner said, was to be diligent and contribute consistently and systematically.

After twenty-five years of doing just that, their next big meeting with a financial planner was an incredible letdown. Barring some drastic measures, they won't be living a millionaire lifestyle in retirement. Instead, their empty-nest years are going to be one big, prolonged sacrifice to meet a magic number.

You've seen the online calculators and read the articles; planners boil retirement down to a magic number. To them, your life and retirement are a simple math problem. Pick a retirement date, how much you'll spend each year, how much you have now, when you'll pass, etc., and do the math to find your "number." That magic number is how much you'll need at the beginning of retirement. The number is the goal, and you have to scrimp and save to retire securely.

Thousands of advisors and countless individuals follow this process.

There's just one problem: Your life is not a number. Attempting to create a great life and retirement using the magic-number technique is like trying to create a masterpiece with a paint-by-numbers kit. You just follow basic, generic instructions:

1. Budget.
2. Maximize the contribution to your 401(k).
3. Contribute to IRAs.
4. Pay off bad debt.
5. Buy our investment products.
6. Save every extra penny you can.

Match the "4" with Kelly green, fill in the bubble, and there you have grass. A few more colors—beige for the fur, cotton-candy pink for the tongue, happy yellow for the sun—and there you have a little kitty basking in a sunlit field.

Sure it's a painting, but is it art? You can hang it on the wall and admire it, but would you? It's not inspiring, it's not creative, and, worst of all, it doesn't represent you. It could be painted by and for anyone.

This paint-by-numbers approach to retirement may have worked for your parents. Their retirement picture was simpler than yours. They worked longer, lived more modestly, and spent less time in retirement than the modern retiree. They had Social Security and, likely, a pension to cover most expenses. Work comprised a big percentage of their lives, and retirement, the smallest percentage. Worn out from work, they enjoyed less-expensive pleasures than modern retirees. Their lives were much more uniform. Paint-by-numbers retirement worked well for most of them.

But you are not your parents. You, the modern retiree, will live a dynamic retirement. A one-dimensional, simple-math–based approach won't work for you, yet it's still the standard advice of most retirement books and financial planners. Your generation will live longer and be more active and more engaged than any generation the world has seen. You live a multidimensional, Technicolor life.

Use this paint-by-numbers approach, and the "answer" to your retirement dreams will most likely seem so big and unattainable, you'll freak out. Working toward it will force you to sacrifice more of your life today to build the massive savings required to make the numbers work. It's simple, scary math for most and provides only bad choices.

Most importantly, using the traditional approach could quite literally cost you your life. No drama here. I've seen it. You'll have to work more hours, save more money, and take more investment risk in an effort to hit your number.

Recently I was talking with my wife about retirement. As a hard-charging IT staffing professional at age 29+undisclosed, her comment about retirement reflects how many of us feel.

"If I can just bust my butt for the next ten years," she said, "I should be able to slow down." I've heard this familiar refrain from clients too. This costly mentality makes you miss out on the only life you have while you work to meet your number.

And the majority won't even think beyond the butt-busting ten years. Most people I encounter, my wife included, focus more on the race than the destination.

The simplicity of paint-by-numbers retirement makes us run too hard—so hard it's easy to forget what we're actually running toward. We just want to catch our breath and get away from the rat race.

I have a client who owns and runs three separate and different businesses. He's so busy running the businesses, he doesn't have time to live. Like this client, we work so hard to earn, raise a family, save, and invest that our *lives* pass us by. And we come by it honestly, because that's what the experts tell us we need to do to prepare for retirement. Put off today so you can be prepared for tomorrow.

And what if you can't hit those savings and investing numbers no matter how hard you work? No worries, paint-by-numbers retirement has an answer: Just plan on settling for less of a life later on. Forget retiring on time; you'll have to work longer. Forget traveling the country in an RV. Forget traveling altogether; you'll probably be struggling to keep up with inflation. With such a large retirement number looming, your entire focus changes along with your life.

Paint-by-numbers retirement forces you to live on less today or settle for less tomorrow. Or maybe even both!

Paint-by-numbers retirement could, quite literally, cost you your life.

Screw that!

You are a baby boomer! You want to rock retirement! Your generation has been redefining American life since you were born. From the cultural revolution in the '60s, the "Me" generation of the '70s, and the yuppies of the '80s to the corporate chiefs of the '90s and empty nesters of today, you've changed the rules all along the way. And you're doing the same for retirement!

Baby boomers entering retirement want more than their parents had. You don't want a gold watch and a moving van to Florida. You want freedom and independence to pursue life on your own terms.

You've worked hard, raised children, and sacrificed; now you want *your* life.

This book is about a modern way to approach retirement, one that one that will help you rock your retirement years. It's about how you can live well today and slowly put in place the freedom to glide into a more independent lifestyle as you retire. It's about starting with a fresh canvas and creating a piece of art you're proud to hang in a prominent position, a piece your children will admire as an example of how to *live*.

It's about taking your wisdom, creativity, and experience and producing something unique to you. Something that reflects what you treasure most. I call it the Retirement Masterpiece. When you get it right, you have something even more valuable than a painting: You have your life.

This Retirement Masterpiece approach takes back the power from the calculator and puts the brush in your hands. Use it, and you'll have a framework to:

- Dream up the life you want (today and tomorrow)
- Easily manage your earning and spending
- Find out what life is possible
- Balance living well today and tomorrow
- Make quicker, more informed decisions to adjust as life unfolds
- Control your financial security
- Live a more balanced life

The Retirement Masterpiece is built for your Technicolor life, the life that you want to live once you've done the "career thing." It factors in more than just the numbers; it helps you focus on creating a life from which you may never retire.

RUNNING TO AND FROM

The tight focus of paint-by-numbers retirement on the financial aspect blurs the details of what life will actually be like once you retire.

Many run away from work rather than into retirement.

"I hate my job."

"I'm traveling too much."

"Why does my boss call me at home?"

"My job is affecting my health!"

"I can't keep up these hours much longer."

"If someone steals my sandwich from the refrigerator again, I'm going to lose it."

Trapped inside the lines, we're tired, worn thin, and the clock can't tick down quickly enough. Retirement is both the focus and the cure, yet when it arrives, it feels hollow. After a few honeymoon months, a sense of being adrift creeps in where the pain of work used to be. Poorly planned retirement can drift you toward boredom and discomfort, and many baby boomers are discovering in retirement that they're not ready for the park bench of life just yet.

Paint-by-numbers retirement centers on moving away from full-time paid work but doesn't address what you're moving toward. It's designed for our grandparents and parents who reached retirement age mentally and physically exhausted. They were near the end of their lives and ready to sit quietly on that park bench.

Today, we feel we're near our prime from an education, experience, and wisdom standpoint. Our entire lives have been about building—a family, a business, and/or a corporate career. We're accustomed to the cycle of setting our sights on a goal, pouring our energy and effort into its achievement, and reaping the rewards. Conventional retirement disrupts that cycle and replaces it with . . . nothingness. As a result, some people become professional shoppers, and others, full-time drinkers, gamblers, or TV watchers. Soon, another game of golf doesn't sound exciting; it sounds just as exhausting as the old job. Unmoored, vitality, excitement, and engagement wane and then disappear.

A Retirement Masterpiece requires you to consider what you're running toward, and position yourself to glide right into it, not only financially, but also mentally. You can bypass the nothingness and transition smoothly into the next phase of life. It can sound complicated, but you don't need a comprehensive laminated twenty-one–point plan. You need only answer one question: "How can I gain more freedom and independence in my life today and tomorrow?"

It's important to note here that I'm not an outsider bashing the financial-planning industry. I am them. Every day I walk life with clients on their journey into and through retirement. I've used the paint-by-numbers retirement model. I've advised people like you throughout my entire career, which began in 1991. In 2001, I received my Certified Financial Planner designation (CFP®) from the Certified Financial Planner Board of Standards, Inc. In 2002, I received the Certified Investment Management Analyst designation (CIMA®) from the Investment Management Consultants Association® in partnership with the Wharton School, the Certified Wealth Management Analyst designation, and the Accredited Investment Fiduciary designation (AIF®).

For a number of years, I taught the Retirement Planning and Employee Benefits section of the CFP® candidate program at the University of Texas at Arlington. I've taught wealth management to adults at Texas Christian University. Each year, I teach at continuing-education events for CPAs and others about retirement and Social Security. Each week, I enjoy the privilege of speaking to thousands of people on the *Retirement Answer Man* podcast, answering questions and discussing the issues they face.

I tell you all this not to brag, but to illustrate that I have a deep understanding of financial planning. And not just a theoretical understanding; it's a deep, battle-hardened, got-the-scars-and-medals understanding. I've done great things and really stupid things, from which I've acquired a lot of wisdom.

As a "classically trained" financial planner, I've come to question the traditional retirement-planning process. As I've learned, applied, and taught during my career, I've come to see how the traditional retirement-planning process isn't working. It remains stuck in the old ways. It fails to adjust to the unique needs of you and your generation.

It's a paint-by-numbers approach, and it isn't doing the job.

What follows in the pages of this book is not theory; it's not an intellectual exercise. I live in the real world and advise real people like you: people who work hard, love their family, and want to build a life they can look back on with pride.

As I've worked with my clients these past twenty-five years, I've walked their lives with them. I don't just helicopter in and give advice. Helping people plan their retirement differently and well is what I do each and every day in my office and on my podcast, *The Retirement Answer Man.* It's a far cry from the product-knowledge and sales-presentation training I received as a newly minted advisor.

WHAT THIS BOOK IS NOT

You will not find specific retirement strategies to "make it all work" or explanations of planning tactics. I won't explain Roth IRA conversions, hedge funds, trading strategies, required minimum distributions, tax rules, estate-planning rules, or other tactical considerations. These tactical issues have been covered time and time again. They're useful when needed and potentially disastrous when not. They're tools—nothing more. Like tools, they should be pulled out of the toolbox only when necessary.

Don't get me wrong, I *love* tactics. I love to consider and use them when the time is right. But they don't come first. You wouldn't take a hammer out and start banging on things if you didn't have a nail to drive, would you? So why talk about and research tactics before you know what kind of life you're trying to build and how you're going to build it?

WHAT THIS BOOK IS

This book is about you making the most of the only life you have. It's about helping you to expand your thinking beyond the restricted paint-by-numbers retirement methods most planners offer. I want you to realize you have more options and more control than that.

Whatever age you are, whatever circumstance you find yourself in, you have an opportunity—an opportunity to dream up an incredible rest of your life. That's what this book is about. It's about breaking free from the bad advice that can rob you of the only life you have. It's about envisioning your ideal life and creating your masterpiece. And it's about how to begin your journey toward this great new stage in your life.

CHAPTER 1
YOU ARE NOT YOUR PARENTS

"The things that make me different
are the things that make me ME."

—PIGLET (A. A. MILNE)

Sigmund stood only five feet eight inches tall and weighed just over 145 pounds. A member of the "Greatest Generation," Ziggy was tough as nails. He grew up poor, worked with his hands from the time he was eleven, and could fix almost anything. He married my grandmother young, and they had their first child—my mother—just before he was drafted into World War II.

He served as a tail gunner in the B-17 Flying Fortress. I recall him telling me that he volunteered for every possible mission so he could get back quickly to his wife and daughter. Was he scared?

"Sure," he said, "but I figured if I was going to go, it didn't matter which flight it was on."

When he returned from the war with a Purple Heart, he worked a variety of jobs to provide for my grandmother and their young family. He made money as a boxer, taxi driver, factory worker, and—finally—as a postal carrier throughout the cold Michigan winters. He did whatever was needed to provide for his family.

My grandmother, Mary, worked hard too. She built a loving household for her three daughters (including one who was mentally disabled), and tailored clothes for her girls and the grandkids. I remember watching her pin paper patterns on cloth to cut, and then sewing all the pieces together. While she deeply loved her sewing machine, my sisters and I were intimidated by it—especially after my sister Joanne ran her finger under the needle.

In the backyard she kept a garden of carrots, zucchini, green beans, and tomatoes. We loved to help pick them with her. She canned preserves and even made her own wine in the basement. She would put her concoction into a big, glass water bottle with a balloon on top, and when the balloon inflated, she'd know the wine was ready. I never got to taste it, but I still remember hearing her sing "Tiny Bubbles" as she cooked her homemade chicken soup in the kitchen. That was when she wasn't working part-time at Minnesota Fabrics for extra money.

There was no money or mentality to outsource the chores of my grandparents' lives. When the house needed cleaning, they cleaned it. If the car broke down, Grandpa fixed it. When the walls needed painting, they painted them. When the grass needed mowing, Grandpa mowed it. And if a project came up that was too big or complicated to handle alone, they called their friends to chip in and figure it out together.

Big fun for my grandparents was playing games. My grandfather taught me to play backgammon and would whip me at it every chance he got. My grandmother taught me to play Michigan Rummy and poker. We'd spend hours playing for pennies. There were no big vacations or eating out; fun was had at home.

Once they retired, they moved to a small home in Florida to escape the cold Michigan winters. Retirement for them was simple. They read more books than I could count, watched television and went to church. A big trip for them was going to the movies. Worn out from saving the world, working with their hands for years, and raising a family on little money, they were ready to sit on the park bench of life and rest in retirement.

If you're a baby boomer, you likely recognize Ziggy and Mary in your parents.

PARK BENCHES AND PLAYGROUNDS

When past generations retired, they found a comfortable bench on the edge of the figurative playground of life and settled in. They were physically tired in the most literal sense. Worn out from fighting wars, engaging in physical labor, and raising families, they were ready to sit. Rarely did they venture out onto the playground of life. When they did, typically it was to play in the safe zones: a trip to Las Vegas or a visit to the grandchildren.

Recently, I was talking with a fifty-five-year-old planning client, Mark, about his plans to retire. We were creating a road map for his retirement at age fifty-six.

"Mark, you're obviously very skilled and have a lot of drive left, what will you do?" I asked.

"Roger, I've given a lot of my life to my company," he replied with confidence. "I'm ready for a life outside of work. I'm ready for a life without the constant drumbeat of projects, deadlines, and meetings. My wife and I are ready to explore life together. We're ready to live our lives."

If you're a baby boomer like Mark, your life is drastically different than your parents' lives. Vast transformations have taken place in just a few decades. The following five changes make absolutely essential the movement from paint-by-numbers retirement to creating a Retirement Masterpiece.

Living Longer in Retirement

I'm guessing if you're reading this book, you already know that you and I, on average, are going to live longer in retirement than our parents did. In 2016, the average age of retirement in the US was sixty-three (Wallace, 2016). Although the average age of retirement hasn't moved much in the past forty years, the amount of time we live in it *has*. According to the Stanford Center on Longevity (SCL), the average number of years men spend in retirement has increased from eight years in 1950 to almost twenty years today. That's a 150 percent increase! It's going to continue to increase, too. If you're sixty today, you have a 50 percent chance of living to age ninety or more. That implies a retirement of thirty-plus years.

When my grandfather retired at the age of sixty-three in 1980, he lived nine years, until the age of seventy-two. The paint-by-numbers retirement approach worked well for him. The math was simple.

We will live a lot longer than that, which means the math gets more complicated. We're going to have a lot of free time on our hands. Spending twenty, thirty, sometimes even forty years in retirement is a reality now, and in the not-too-distant future, it may be even longer. As exciting (or scary) as that is, it creates retirement-planning issues that paint-by-numbers can't address.

Living Healthier

"Wait a second," you say. "Healthier?" *Time* magazine recently reported, "American baby boomers are more stressed, less healthy, and have slightly less health care coverage than people in the same age group did a decade ago." So how can I say "healthier"?

It's true; studies show that baby boomers, as a whole, aren't so healthy. It's a big problem. When I say "healthier," I mean *focused* on being healthier. Most of our health issues are self-inflicted, and more often we're recognizing this and doing something about it. We've realized we're going to live longer and have decided we want to be healthy enough to make the most of it. And unlike our parents' generation, there's plenty of help.

Here's a good example: Not long ago, a fifty-five-year-old couple I work with went on a cruise up the Rhine. Each day, the boat stopped along the river so they could spend the day exploring the ancient cities by foot. It took a lot of walking, and the husband's knees ached the entire trip. Afterward, sitting in my office, we discussed their vision for their retirement.

As he told me the story of their trip, he said, "Heck if I'm not healthy enough to enjoy retirement with my wife! We've worked years for this moment, and I'm not going to miss it."

In that meeting they set action items to meet with an orthopedic surgeon and to start eating healthier. As of this writing, he's had one knee replaced, and he and his wife have each lost ten pounds.

This is our reality. We may not have always had the healthiest habits (I'm looking in the mirror now with a frown), but we're committed to living healthier to make the most of the only life we have. We're taking advantage of all the advancements in health and fitness to invest in our well-being.

In addition, recent studies have shown that although longevity is increasing, morbidity is compressing. Morbidity refers to health-related quality of life before death. In their book *The 100-Year Life,* professors Lynda Gratton and Andrew Scott discuss this point: "In the twenty years between 1984 and 2004, the number of people aged 85–89 who were classified as disabled fell from 22 percent to 12 percent, and for those aged over 95, from 52 percent to 31 percent. Older people seem to be fitter and also can achieve more as technology and public support improve."

So not only will you live longer, you'll also live healthier as technology and public support improve.

Being More Active

We'll have a more active lifestyle in retirement than our parents. Retirement wasn't a chance to live; it was a chance to rest. Compare that to Jim. Jim is fifty-four, and, as a result of a successful career in IT and careful planning, he'll retire at age fifty-six.

During one meeting I asked him, "Jim, what are you going to do with your time? You'll be fifty-six with a lot of energy and passion left in the tank."

He pulled out a piece of paper. On it he had listed thirty-five things he and his wife wanted to do during retirement. Here are a few:

- Help run the local Junior Achievement chapter
- His wife, Mary, wanted to mentor young professional women
- Be a bigger part of their grandchildren's lives
- Teach a parenting class together at church
- Travel to each continent
- Help out at the local entrepreneur center

No park bench for Jim and Mary. Retirement for them isn't a time to go rest; it's an opportunity to gain freedom and independence from corporate life in order to dedicate time to their passions.

I confirmed this desire for independence and freedom a few years ago on my podcast, *The Retirement Answer Man*. For five months, I invited listeners onto the show to share their journey toward retirement. Each week, I'd interview a listener, asking him about his journey and what he wanted for the future. When I asked about his concept of retirement, a common theme echoed on each show: the time to pursue passions. Men and women alike wanted freedom from the daily grind of full-time work to pursue their own interests. Each interest was unique. They included:

- Start a business
- Teach
- Travel
- Serve
- Consult
- Compete (racing, riding, sailing, running, swimming, trivia)
- Create (knitting, woodworking, glassblowing, painting, writing, dancing, music)
- Focus on relationships
- Do work for enjoyment, not obligation

Before we move on, it's important I point out that sitting on the park bench is still part of retirement. As one podcast listener put it, "Roger, I earned the right to rest. During my career, I traveled the world many times and missed out on many little things. Retirement for me will be about living a slow-paced life." Creating a Retirement Masterpiece allows for exactly that.

Being More Connected

We don't write letters anymore; we post status updates. We post cute dog videos and selfies from our latest adventures. We use social media to stay connected to friends and family. Baby boomers are the fastest-growing segment of Facebook and the biggest users (Lockard 2015). From our PC—Mac, for me—and smartphone, we're able to glimpse into the lives of those we care about and connect with friends everywhere. We don't place long-distance phone calls; we Skype or FaceTime for free with family and friends across the world.

We're wired!

Our parents and grandparents, on the other hand, lived a local life. They watched local news and read the local papers. They talked about what was happening down the street or in their city. They watched the world from the local mall and on television.

They had local friends. The people they played cards or watched the game with were friends from the neighborhood, church, or the local lodge. It was harder then to stay connected with people who lived elsewhere. Catching up with family or friends meant long-distance phone calls during off-hours to keep the charges down (remember those?). Flying to visit family or friends was a really big deal.

They had local activities. They sewed, tended gardens, worked on cars, did crafts, and cooked. Their hobbies revolved around their local community. Their neighborhood, church, or lodge was the center of activity. Walks to the park, lunches at the local diner, and club meetings at church were trips "out."

Many accuse social media of pulling people out of life and into the computer. However, for baby boomers, social sites like Facebook and Meetup have allowed them to stay connected to faraway friends and connect with others who have similar interests.

Take John, for example. John liked to ride his bicycle two to three times a week on the country roads near his home. For years he rode alone, until he started posting his rides on Strava, an app which tracks your rides and compares you to others who ride the same roads. One day while riding, he came alongside another cyclist and chatted for a bit. Subsequently, they connected via the Strava app and discovered that they rode similar routes each week. Now, a year later, he and Ralph have a cadre of local friends who ride together.

Or take Sally. When she retired, she reconnected with past friends on Facebook. At first they just peeked into each other's life via status updates. Then they started to comment on each other's posts. This led to phone calls, which lead to group video chats, which ultimately led to annual trips.

People with similar interests are connecting more and more online and meeting locally. Whatever your interest, it's getting easier to find others who share the same passion. Whether you're a cyclist, runner, knitter, brewer, or virtually any hobbyist, social media allows you to find and connect with others who enjoy similar pursuits.

Being Experience Focused

As we saw, the Stanford Center on Longevity report showed a 150 percent increase in the number of years spent in retirement. What isn't captured in that statistic is that when we retire, we're more educated, skilled, connected, mobile, and engaged than any generation in history. In short, we still have fuel in our tanks, and we're not content with small, local experiences.

We view the freedom and independence gained during retirement as our ticket to live life on our own terms. It's an opportunity to become more active, to go out and explore and create the experiences we didn't have the freedom to pursue while working.

Unlike our parents, we have the money and the mentality to outsource most chores. There is little time or inclination to mow the yard or clean the house. There are things to do and places to go!

We are *experience* focused. We rent RVs and explore the country. We serve on boards and consult for companies. We start businesses around our hobbies or passions. We fly across the country and around the world. We go back to school and back to exploring our passions. There's no time to sit on the park bench or sing "Tiny Bubbles" like my grandma. We're too busy getting dirty romping around the playground.

I have a client whom I'll call Susan. She's seventy-four years old. Susan spends her summers living on the shore of Lake Michigan, and her winters, in Texas. She travels with friends to watch PGA tournaments. She doesn't cook much and eating out at nice restaurants is one of her hobbies. Her husband passed away eight years ago, and she's had three or four boyfriends since then.

And then there's Jack; he's sixty-eight. He retired at age sixty. After a brief honeymoon of rest, Jack was ready for action. He realized pretty quickly that although he enjoyed the slower pace of life, he needed to stay active. He connected with a company that placed him on consulting assignments for the very company from which he retired. From time to time, they'd contact him with an offer. If the project interested him and fit his schedule, he'd take it. If it didn't, he would decline. He did interesting projects off and on for twelve years until he stopped to spend time with his young grandkids. For Jack, this was the best of both worlds. He was able to earn income and take assignments that interested him, and still have the free time to pursue his passions.

Susan and Jack are not anomalies. They represent the new reality of retirement. Every time I survey my podcast audience, I find the chief desire of retirees is the freedom to pursue life more on their own terms. They may sit on the park bench from time to time, but they're out on the playground of life mixing it up as well. A paint-by-numbers retirement is no longer relevant to them.

As you'll see, not only is it no longer relevant, using it could cost you your life.

CHAPTER SUMMARY

☐ **Living Longer**—The trend toward longer lives has been consistently higher for over one hundred years. A sixty-year-old today has a 50 percent chance of living to age ninety or greater. A twenty-year-old today has a 50 percent chance of living to age one hundred or greater.

☐ **Living Healthier**—Our parents were worn out from more physical work and less-advanced health care. As a result of rapidly advancing technology and services, health-conscious retirees will stay healthier and independent longer.

☐ **Being More Active**—Our parents lived much less active retirements. Baby boomers view retirement as their chance to finally do the things they enjoy. Modern retirees go into retirement ready to do more.

☐ **Being More Connected**—Our parents led local lives. Technology and the Internet have expanded the lives of baby boomers in retirement.

☐ **Being Experience Focused**—Our parents rested on park benches during retirement. Baby boomers are out enjoying life and changing the world.

CHAPTER 2
THE PROBLEM WITH TRADITIONAL RETIREMENT PLANNING

"We cannot solve our problems with the same
kind of thinking we used to create them."

—ALBERT EINSTEIN

M y first car was a 1972 Volkswagen Karmann Ghia. It was 1982. I was a sophomore in high school, and I was driving. I was cool, 'cause anyone who drove was cool. You'd think having a Karmann Ghia would make me extra cool, but it didn't. It was rusty, with no heat or air-conditioning, and I lived in Michigan. In the winters, I'd drive while scraping frost off the inside of the windows. On icy roads, the car would drift regardless of how I turned the wheel. Even though it looked cool, it was not that fun to drive; it wasn't reliable, and at times it could be outright dangerous.

I recall going on a date one Saturday night. As Kim and I were driving to the theater, we suddenly heard a big *CLUNK* and then a loud scraping noise. When I looked in my rearview mirror, I saw a stream of sparks making a rooster tail like a speedboat. I slowly pulled over and got out to see what had happened. The right side of my bumper was resting on the pavement, bent out from the car. As my lovely date waited patiently in the car, I sifted through the garbage in my trunk, found a cord and was able to secure the bumper to the car. It was bad enough that I was dirty and sweaty, but when I returned to the car, my lovely date wasn't so lovely anymore. She was hot and sweaty and not too thrilled with her choice of going out with me. We finally made it to the movie, and I was able to take her home without incident. It was a memorable experience for all the wrong reasons.

Paint-by-numbers retirement is a lot like my old Karmann Ghia. It was cool when it was originally created, but it's showing its age. It's rusty and missing modern features necessary to get you where you want to go in comfort.

Since your retirement will be different than your parents', it makes sense that the way you plan should be different, as well. But it's not different, and that's a problem. Having used and taught the traditional approach for years, I have come to see that it paralyzes clients more than it inspires them. Retirement plans don't inspire action. The avalanche of financial charts, graphs, and projections buried in pages of disclosures end up sitting on a shelf collecting dust.

As the host of the *Retirement Answer Man* podcast, I have unique access to the experiences and concerns of people like you who are seeking answers and making plans for the second half of their lives. If you're like most people nearing retirement, you're deeply concerned about how you'll survive the rush of risks that could derail not just your retirement, but also your life. Inflation, health-care costs, taxes, longevity, bear markets, rising interest rates, long-term care, and countless other unknowns loom over your head as you move toward retirement.

To compound the problem, many have lost confidence—rightly so—in the financial industry's ability to guide us there safely. High-pressure sales tactics and high-profile scandals make it difficult to know whom to trust.

What are we to do?

WHY YOU DON'T GET THE ADVICE YOU NEED

It might help you to know how we got here, how paint-by-numbers retirement became the norm. The financial-planning industry is not really very old. Prior to the 1970s, mostly wealthy people invested. People like you and I didn't have much money, if any, in the markets. The wealthy invested primarily to preserve and grow wealth they created through their work. Investing for them was primarily a preserver of wealth, a vehicle to generate income, keep up with inflation, and slowly grow over time.

In 1974, Congress passed the Employee Retirement Income Security Act (ERISA), and everything changed. It brought about the democratization of investing by introducing the Individual Retirement Arrangement (IRA). In 1978, the section of the Internal Revenue Code that made 401(k) plans possible was enacted. Thus began a massive transition from pensions to 401(k)s and IRAs. "In the US, the number of employees with access to defined benefit plans declined from 62 percent in 1983 to 17 percent by 2013" (Gratton and Scott 2016). Slowly, you and I became responsible for our own retirement, and the financial-services industry sprang up to help. This was the start of a big shift in mind-set. Investing became less about preserving wealth generated from work and industry, and more about creating wealth. *Investing* became the engine of wealth creation, instead of *us*.

The financial-advice industry exploded in the 1980s and 1990s as assets moved into 401(k) plans and IRAs invested in stocks and bonds. The number of mutual funds offered went from approximately 594 in 1980 to over 8,000 in 2000. During that same time, the assets in mutual funds went from $134 billion to nearly $7 trillion (Investment Company Institute 2014). Average daily volume on the New York Stock Exchange went from 6.9 million shares a day in the 1960s to 19.5 million in the 1970s to 109 million in the 1980s and 386 million in the 1990s (NYSE 2017). Along with the volume came financial-news channels like CNBC and magazines like *Money*. Financial planners ostensibly showed their clients how to use a little money invested over time to potentially make a lot—how to create wealth through investing. I was one of them. I remember showing mountain charts illustrating how much you'd have to put in your 401(k) to have the potential to retire as a millionaire. People began to regard investing as the primary source of wealth rather than themselves. The focus of retirement shifted from the individual to his or her investments. The human became lost in the pie chart. As we became totally dependent on investing, it created a huge overarching worry about maintaining lifestyle and running out of money. We gave away our power. Our investments controlled our wealth and future, not us.

The professions of financial planning and retirement planning came from the investment and insurance industries. Until the recent advent of financial-planning–degree programs at the university level, financial planners came from the sales force in these industries. Pause for a second: sales force. They created the industry; they set the standards.

Tens of millions of dollars have been spent by major financial firms on advertising to convince you that your financial advisor is on par with your CPA or attorney, that he or she is your "trusted advisor" and able to help you manage your entire financial life. The truth is, although almost all advisors are well-intentioned and capable, they don't have the skill set or training to think beyond investment solutions. Unlike an attorney or a CPA, a financial planner doesn't receive deep technical training. While aspiring attorneys delve into huge law books and CPAs dive into the tax code, the aspiring financial advisor digs into sales and investment-product knowledge.

At one time, I worked for a major New York-based investment firm. When I joined, I spent three intensive weeks training in New York. Guess what I learned? Sales presentation and investment-product knowledge. Once I returned to the office, ongoing training consisted of lunches and workshops on planning strategies wrapped in investment products.

Your longer, more active lifestyle and desire to live well now as well as later has changed the dynamics of planning. Unfortunately, the majority of financial firms that invent and sell financial products as a solution haven't learned how to help you address the issues you face. Instead, they've created more complicated and expensive products to sell you. This is the hammer that's used over and over to nail you into paint-by-numbers retirement, a one-dimensional solution.

THE SAVINGS-GAP TRAP

The financial-planning industry has a well-defined process. It's the standard for retirement planning and the one I taught students as part of the process of becoming a Certified Financial Planner. It's a well-thought-out process that, regrettably, is mostly applied in a paint-by-numbers way. If you go through this sausage grinder, your life could be caught in what I call the "savings gap trap." To understand how this happens, it's best to show you.

Here are the Financial Planning Practice Standards developed and published by the Certified Financial Planner Board of Standards (CFP Board, 2017):

1. Establishing and defining the relationship with a client
2. Gathering client data
3. Analyzing and evaluating the client's financial status
4. Developing and presenting financial-planning recommendations

5. Implementing the financial-planning recommendations

6. Monitoring

It is a well-designed process, unfortunately all too often applied by advisors who were only taught how to sell and implement investment products. Now let's demonstrate how it plays out. Tell me if it sounds familiar.

Step One: Establishing and Defining the Relationship with a Client

Mr. and Mrs. Jones decide they need a plan for retirement. They get a recommendation from a friend and go meet with the planner. When they meet Mr. Financial Planner, he asks lots and lots of questions and talks a lot about his expertise and the capabilities of his firm. The guy is super nice, seems really smart, and a friend referred them to him, so Mr. and Mrs. Jones agree to start the process.

Step Two: Gathering Client Data

Once the relationship is established, Mr. and Mrs. Jones enter the data-gathering step. This torturous step requires that they complete a questionnaire asking for, well, everything. This includes such things as:

1. When do they want to retire?

2. How much money will they spend during retirement?

3. What investment assets do they have now?

4. What is their current investment allocation?

5. What income sources do they have now?

6. Will they have a pension? If so, how much?

7. How much Social Security will they receive?

In addition, Mr. and Mrs. Jones complete a risk-tolerance questionnaire (more on this in a future chapter). Mr. Financial Planner uses all the data and crunches the numbers to tell the Joneses if their present financial status is sufficient to give them what they need down the road. These calculations take into account inflation, expected investment return rates, tax rates, and a timetable for implementing any plans and changes—i.e., the retirement date.

A quick stop here. If you've used a financial planner, you've experienced the dreaded "data gathering" phase. Remember that fifty-page questionnaire? In my career, I'm ashamed to admit that I've subjected clients to the torture of asking for definitive answers on what they want to do and spend decades into the future. No range will do. I couldn't put "range" into my calculator; I needed a hard number. I've subjected them to compiling and reviewing ALL their financial information in two- to three-hour meetings. You know who you are, and I'm so, so sorry.

Step Three: Analyzing and Evaluating the Client's Financial Status

This is where the analysis begins. Now that Mr. and Mrs. Jones have provided reams of paper on every aspect of their financial life and exact guestimates on what they want for retirement, Mr. Planner can run the data to discover the number needed at retirement to fully fund their goals. He'll enter data like:

- Retirement date and life expectancy

- Spending goals

- Investment assets

- Current asset allocation

- Risk-tolerance score

- Current savings rate

- Other assets and liabilities

- Future income sources

Once he's determined their magic number, he'll develop a target asset allocation aligned with their risk tolerance and determine if they're on track to hit their retirement number. If they're not on track, which is almost always the case, Mr. Planner will develop investment recommendations to help close the gap.

Step Four: Developing and Presenting Financial-Planning Recommendations

In this step, Mr. Planner develops and presents recommendations to fill the savings gap between the clients' "magic number" and the assets they expect to have, and recommends appropriate investment and/or insurance vehicles to help them save and raise the necessary capital for their retirement years.

Step Five: Implementing the Financial-Planning Recommendations

Mr. Financial Planner pulls in as many assets as he can and implements the plan.

Step Six: Monitoring

Mr. Financial Planner calls the Jones family maybe once a year.

This well-thought-out process applied by financial advisors, focused mainly on saving and investing, almost always creates a savings gap. That's the trap! Given how long you'll likely live and how active you'll be, this simple math usually traps you into nothing but bad choices.

Paint-by-numbers planning worked for your parents' simpler life, but it doesn't work for you. You're not your parents, and staying within the lines can set you up for some really bad choices. Use this process, and you'll likely find out you're *far* behind having what you need. The probability of reaching your goals ain't so good, because once your "savings gap" is identified, the financial planner is trained to prescribe additional savings and investments in order to fill the gap. This means less money for your current life and more money to your 401(k), Roth IRA or other savings account. Often this also means more investment risk (to get the needed returns), which means more ups and downs for you to suffer through.

The bottom line: Sacrifice more of your life now.

Don't like that option? Want to keep your current lifestyle or just can't squeeze one more penny out of the budget?

OK, traditional planning has another option for you. If you'd rather not (or cannot) save more or take on more investment risk, we can adjust your retirement goals to make the numbers work. You'll be able to live better today, but be prepared to live less of the life you want later on down the road.

"OK, Mr. and Mrs. Jones, what will it be? Sacrifice today or tomorrow? Or how about a little bit of both?"

No wonder only 24 percent of baby boomers say they are confident they will have enough money to last their lifetime (Corbin 2016). Caught in the savings-gap trap of "save more, invest more" math, many leave meetings with a financial planner feeling discouraged. They wonder, *How will I save more when there's not much left at the end of each month?* and *Is my retirement totally dependent on my investments?* Dispirited, they either:

- Lower their current lifestyle to save and invest more
- Decide they'll just settle for less later in life
- Take a lot of investment risk in hopes the markets will bail them out
- Throw up their hands and leave their lives to fate
- Or do a bit of all of the above.

Save more, invest more, or settle for less can't be the only choices.

YOUR LIFE IS MORE THAN A MATH PROBLEM

Read almost any personal-finance magazine or website, and you'll likely find an article on the dismal state of preparedness for retirement. Experts harp on how you're not saving enough, not budgeting enough or not investing enough. These experts aren't completely off base; they're just thinking inside the lines of the paint-by-numbers retirement model. Like most financial planners, they view your life as a math problem that can only be solved by "save more, invest more" math or settling for less.

By using that paradigm, of course there'll be a savings gap! Your life during retirement will be so much longer and dynamic than past generations. The mountain of savings needed to cover the cost of a thirty- to forty-year retirement in which you'll be active is an almost insurmountable number. "Save more, invest more" doesn't work anymore, but financial planners still use the same equation to come up with the set of bad possibilities from which they force you to choose between sacrificing your life today in order to save, sacrificing your life tomorrow, or a bit of both.

Here's an example. Take Bill and Mary. They're fifty years old and have two kids in college. Let's use a retirement calculator I found on a major financial firm's website to do the math. Here are the facts:

Combined income: $150,000
Total Retirement Savings: $400,000
Current savings rate: $40,000 (26 percent of their income)
Desired retirement spending: $100,000
Desired retirement age: Sixty-three
Investment profile: Moderate

According to the calculator, to achieve their goal, Bill and Mary will need to save a whopping $1,051,400 over the next thirteen years. That's over $80,000 per year! That's in addition to what they're already saving.

Here are the suggestions given to get them on track, verbatim:

- Change your retirement age to sixty-nine.
- Increase your annual retirement contribution to $88,400.
- Reduce your spending while in retirement to $61,000 per year.
- Investigate some options and ideas for retirement savings.

Talk to a xxxxx consultant about your next steps. Call XXX-XXX-XXXX.

See the choices? Settle for less today in order to save, or settle for less tomorrow; oh, and by the way, it still may not work.

I'm not trying to beat this to death here; well, actually I *am*, because your life is too important. I've seen too many people resign themselves to these horrible choices, too many people miss out on their life as they stress out about the future, too many people choose not to plan in order to avoid this crazy math. Some postpone life now for the false promise of security and happiness later. Others throw their hands in the air, live for today, and do nothing to take care of their future, the retirement version of "YOLO" (you only live once).

BALANCING YOUR TEETER-TOTTER

Remember the teeter-totter at your neighborhood playground? You and a friend would sit on opposite ends and bounce up and down. When I was a kid without a teeter-totter partner (so sad), I'd stand on the middle of the board with one foot on each side and try to balance. I'd spread my hands like a surfer and wobble back and forth, shifting my weight to keep the board balanced off the ground. It was the closest I could come to surfing a big wave in Michigan.

Your life is like that. When you're making decisions about money and life, you do the same thing. One end of the teeter-totter is today; the other is tomorrow. With every choice you make to save or spend, to work or play, to eat well or splurge, you're trying to balance your teeter-totter. You're trying to live a great life right now, and have a great life later on. Paint-by-numbers retirement asks you to keep one side of the teeter-totter on the ground.

Missing Life

I grew up in a single-parent home. My parents divorced when I was three, leaving my mom the sole breadwinner of the family. She took her responsibilities seriously, believing her first duty was to provide an income to put a roof over our heads and food on the table. That's where she focused all of her energy.

When I was a teen and beginning to think about the future, my mom and I had many conversations about the value of living today versus living for tomorrow. I was young and naive and completely into living in the moment. The imaginary future didn't require my attention. "Seize the day!" I would exclaim. She, on the other hand, argued that it was necessary to delay gratification for more important priorities. I remember her telling me that when we get older, we must take on more responsibility. She missed much of the richness of life while preparing for the future.

She talked about slowing down someday. She talked about relaxing in retirement. She talked about traveling. She talked about these things as she worked full time in a business she didn't love, even earning a law degree in service to her work as she mothered my sisters and me.

Sadly, that time of relaxation never came. My mom developed cancer and died at the age of forty-eight. All her dreams to "slow down and live someday" vanished. She missed weddings, grandchildren, and the chance to live *her* life. It broke my heart. Her sharp focus on living for tomorrow caused her to miss out on the only life she had.

I've seen this same mind-set in people faced with the amount of savings required under a paint-by-numbers retirement plan. They buckle down. They work more. They forego vacations. They say no to life. They plow every extra penny into their 401(k) and taxable investment accounts, running to close the savings-gap mountain on the chart their advisor showed them. Like my mom, they miss out on their life.

YOLO (You Only Live Once)

I've seen the opposite too. Faced with an insurmountable savings gap, I've seen families give up on tomorrow. Rather than intentionally plan their life and financial future, they choose instead to enjoy today and deal with tomorrow . . . tomorrow.

I recall one gentleman in particular. After the 2007–2009 Great Recession, he lost faith. He had no growth to show for years of investing faithfully. He recalled with disgust the mountain chart his advisor had shown him years ago—the chart that illustrated how his nest egg would grow into millions as he neared retirement. He felt betrayed, betrayed by his advisor, by the markets, and by an industry that told him saving and investing was his only answer.

He cashed out his investment accounts, paid off his debts, and said he was going to enjoy himself while he was still healthy. Retirement would just have to take care of itself. In some ways, who could blame him? He had no confidence in either the markets or the advice industry whose process focused only on saving and investing.

Most aren't as extreme as he was. Most people go along half-heartedly with the traditional planning process. They save and invest, but the process doesn't inspire them. They hope it works out, but are trying not to count on it.

It's Time for an Upgrade

Using a Karmann Ghia-like process on your road to retirement isn't a great idea. It was great in its time, but is obsolete on today's road to retirement. It's missing modern safety features and lacks modern onboard computing to help navigate today's complex environment.

It's time for an upgrade. It's time for a new process, one that places the power of your future back in your own hands and doesn't destroy your life in order to get to, and through, retirement.

The rest of this book is about the process I've developed over twenty-five years of walking life with clients. It's not perfect, but nothing is. It focuses not just on saving and investing, but on all aspects of your life. It focuses on helping you create a great life today while still feeling confident about your tomorrow. The first step is to reimagine what your life and retirement can be.

CHAPTER SUMMARY

☐ **Why You Don't Get the Advice You Need**—Most financial advisors were trained in two areas: investment-product knowledge and sales skills. As a result, the paint-by-numbers approach to personal finance focuses on saving and investing. Financial media does the same.

☐ **The Savings-Gap Trap**—The Certified Financial Planner Board of Standards has a well-defined process for retirement planning. When applied using only a saving and investing mind-set, it leads to the savings-gap trap, a snare that creates poor choices.

☐ **Your Life Is More Than a Math Problem**—The paint-by-numbers approach will only lead you to bad choices.

☐ **Balancing Your Teeter-Totter**—Life is about creating a great life today while taking care of your tomorrow.

CHAPTER 3
HOW TO RETHINK YOUR RETIREMENT

"It's never too late to be the person you
know you could have become."

—DAN MILLER, AUTHOR AND COACH

f the truth is that retirement isn't how we're told to imagine it
and normal financial-planning advice leads us on a path offering
only bad choices, how do you create a great life? How do you
rock retirement?

It's time to reimagine your retirement. It's time to stop blindly
believing that just saving and investing more is the answer.

THE FREEDOM FACTOR

Over my years walking with clients on their journey toward retirement, a common theme has emerged. When I helped clients define and plan for retirement, their interest seemed forced. Retirement was something they were "supposed" to plan for, but it didn't hold a lot of excitement for them, even for those in their late fifties.

When asked to define their retirement goals, passion was missing from their voices. They'd say something like, "I guess retiring at sixty-three would be a good target, don't you think?" as though they were randomly pulling it from the air. Or they'd focus on a number, "Once I hit X amount, I'll be set. I just have to suck it up and bust my butt until then."

I found that when I talked with clients about their lives, their eyes were alive. They'd talk about how they'd like to spend more time with their teenage children before they move out or how they'd like to experience more of life while they're healthy. They'd talk about the hobby or passion they'd like to make more time for. The more the focus shifted to actual life, the more engaged they would become. One client put it particularly well. She said, "You build and you build and you build. When you're finished, you're just left with nothing to do. It's not retirement I want; it's the freedom to pursue the things I care about."

That's it, right there. Do you see it? Retirement isn't the goal. The goal is more freedom to pursue the things you're passionate about. I can just hear Cheech saying, "Retirement? We don't need no stinkin' retirement. We need freedom!!"

The listeners of my *Retirement Answer Man* podcast echo this as well. When I surveyed thousands of listeners, an overwhelming 54 percent valued freedom above all else. It's not about reaching the peak of the mountain, getting the gold watch, and stopping. The modern retiree values freedom—freedom to pursue and develop what he or she wants to build.

Unlike our parents, when we reach "normal" retirement age, we're at the top of our game. We've got connections. We've got experience. We've got the hard-earned wisdom and maturity that only comes with time. We're not worn out from physical labor. We're at our peak and still have energy to pursue the things we actually care about. **The key then is to reimagine retirement as a stage of life in which you gain freedom to pursue the things about which you are truly passionate.**

RETIREMENT IS NOT A DATE; IT'S A RELATIONSHIP

Remember dating in high school? You'd spy that gal passing in the hall and start to think about her all the time. Maybe you'd meet her in a group, exchange a few awkward words, and leave thinking she's the "coolest person ever." You'd obsess about her and go way out of your way to be around her.

Once you had worked up the nerve to ask her on a date (I hardly ever got to this point), you'd obsess anew about making your first date great. Is the car clean? Does this shirt look good on me? Hey, can I borrow your deodorant? How's my hair? How's my breath? Is my zipper up?

I was in eighth grade when I first asked a girl to go "steady." She was fairly new in school and although we didn't have any classes together, we'd pass each other in the hall. It started with casual eye contact as we passed, then moved to cautious smiles; if I smile, will she smile back? One day as we passed, I said "Hi." She said "Hi" back, and my world exploded. SHE SAID "HI" BACK! A few weeks later, and we were exchanging whole sentences in the hallway. Finally, I built up the nerve to pop the question I'd been obsessing over ever since that first "hi." One February day in 1980, as we passed in the hall, I blurted out, "Will you go steady with me?" and ran away. The next day, I received a one-word note from her through a friend. It read simply, "Yes."

Later that year, we finally got to have a full conversation at the school dance. Guess what? We didn't have much in common, and it ended right there. In all fairness, there was no way she could have lived up to the relationship I had developed in my head. The bigger the buildup, the bigger the letdown.

Working toward retirement is a bit like this. I'm always amazed by how quickly a client will switch from loving work without a thought of leaving to "I'm ready to get out of this rat race." We think our life focus shifts gradually, but it doesn't. Instead, we have a moment, an event, which changes how we view ourselves and the world. Once this happens with retirement, we begin to idealize it, obsess about it. We think it will be the cure for what ails us.

Phil and Nora are a great example of this type of thinking. They were a couple in their early fifties who lived in central Michigan. Once a month, they'd travel three hours to spend the weekend at their lake house. They both had high-stress jobs, and these weekends were special. They provided both the physical and mental space for them to reconnect, enjoy nature, and unwind.

Once their youngest entered his junior year in college, Phil and Nora changed. They'd raised their family and provided for them; they'd done their job, and now they could focus on themselves. Suddenly, the exciting challenges of work became a headache. The three-hour drive to their lake house seemed longer and longer. *Why not just live up here?* they wondered.

They met with their financial planner (a close friend of mine) and created a plan to retire early, sell their home, and live full-time at their lake house. The plan would require four years of hard work. During those years, Phil and Nora didn't get to spend much time at their lake house. Instead, they worked long hours, traveled more for work, and plowed every extra dollar into their plan.

They did it! They retired in their mid-fifties. They sold their home in town and moved to the lake house. Phil and Nora's first year at the lake house was heaven. They settled into a routine. Each morning they'd walk around the neighborhood, and then Phil would work on improvements he had been planning to do for years. He refinished their deck, hung a porch swing, and painted. Nora hunted thrift shops for old furniture she'd refinish and bring back to life. They'd spend the evenings on the water or at a local diner.

A year later, my advisor friend John visited them to see how retirement was going. After reviewing "the plan" with them, Phil and John sat on the new deck Phil had built, and relaxed.

John said, "So, Phil, you and Nora did it. You raised two great kids, busted your butt saving and investing, and retired early. Congratulations! How does it feel?"

Phil took a sip of his beer and pondered the question.

To John's surprise, Phil replied, "There are days I have done everything I can think to do by ten o'clock in the morning. Then I drink a beer, eat some peanuts, and think, *What happens now?"*

Here's how my advisor friend described it: "I realized I had helped them figure out their money, but not what the money was *for*. I'd helped them with numbers but had failed to address the critical psychological and social aspects of life."

Life is not mechanical, but we tend to treat it that way when we choose to retire. You're not a machine that is retired once your useful life is exhausted. You know that's what the word "retire" means, right? It means taking something out of service because it was too old to be useful. Is that you? I don't think so.

There is no on/off switch moving you from one stage of life to another; rather, it is like a dimmer switch. **Gliding into retirement turns down the static of what we *have* to do, while simultaneously turning up the symphony of the things we *want* to do.**

Retirement is a relationship, one where you ease out of your traditional workaholic life and into a life filled with more freedom and control. Once you've gotten the education, the job, the promotions, and the marriage, and you've had kids, raised them, and put them through college, you're ready to redesign life around *you*. It doesn't happen overnight; just like a great relationship, it takes time.

When I talk to people about retirement, it's often expressed in terms of a date. "I will retire in five and a half years." "I'll retire at sixty-three." "I'll retire when I have $2.2 million in my 401(k)." Retirement is reduced to a date and a dollar amount. It is a specific set of criteria to be met. That's how traditional retirement sells the dream. Once you've colored in the boxes, it's done. It's a light switch. Hit the date or the monetary target, and flip the switch.

Rather than view retirement as a stark, static black-and-white photo, it's helpful to think of it as a gradual change in the landscape. It is the steady progress that allows for joy today and tomorrow. It is gradually dialing into a slower pace now, and building toward a more independent future. It requires a complete shift away from the purely financial aspects to a holistic mind-set, one that incorporates new thinking about health, relationships, purpose, and growth.

SIMPLIFY AND REIMAGINE

The summer Hannah graduated from high school, Bill and Sally were feeling a bit guilty because they were excited about their new season of life. Hannah was their youngest, and the prospect of her moving out was, well, exciting. Sure, they were going to miss her and her sister Julie, but they were just as excited to reimagine their life as a couple. They'd poured their hearts and time into the girls and were excited to see them blossom as adults. Their friends told them how hard the transition would be, but Bill and Sally knew the girls were ready to enter this new phase of life.

The day the kids are out of the house, the "job" of raising the family slows. Now that they're on their own, you can:

- Clean up the house (and it will stay clean).
- Own nice things again.
- Buy the food you want (and it won't get gobbled up).
- Clean the kitchen (and it will stay clean).
- Turn the lights off (and they'll stay off).
- Fill up the car (and it will have gas every time you get in it).
- Put the dishes away (and not find cups everywhere).
- Lock the doors (and they'll stay locked).
- Rest assured the razor, hair product, makeup, shoes, clothes, cologne, and tools won't get permanently "borrowed."

Kids are great, but when your job of raising them is winding down, you enter a new season of discovering yourself and each other again. You turn back to you and your future. You begin to reimagine what life you'll build. This can be a bit scary, but if done right, it can be super exciting.

During this phase of life, you can "right size" your life. This can include selling off things you acquired over the years as your kids moved through the phases of childhood. When our kids moved out, we sold and gave away bags full of clothes, bicycles, skateboards, gaming consoles, furniture, and even a pool table. It felt great to declutter and bring some order to our home. It also helped us reimagine how we use our home. No longer is our game room cluttered with Xbox games, it is now my podcast studio.

Many in this phase discover they have too much house. The home they built to provide a great environment for kids and their activities suddenly feels like overkill. The upkeep of a large home drains resources and time that could be spent on more important things.

One couple I know sold their 3,000-square-foot suburban home and virtually everything in it. They used the funds from the sale to purchase a condo in a college town and the furniture to go in it, and started over. Now they live in 900 square feet, steps away from their offices, trails, coffee shops, restaurants, and shops. Instead of focusing on upkeep and their commute, they focus on friends and experiences.

Another couple plans to sell everything and live in one of those tiny houses. Those are *really* tiny houses—under one thousand square feet. Personally, I can't imagine doing this, but they can! Still another couple plans to maintain their home as an oasis for their large family—a place for everyone to gather and stay connected.

My wife and I currently dream of keeping our home but living in different areas for extended periods. We'd like to immerse ourselves in communities but still have a home base—six months in Franklin, Tennessee; then home; then three months in northern Michigan.

"Right sizing" your home, possessions, spending, and finances allows you to focus on what you want. Hobbies you've put aside to attend your kids' sporting events and recitals catch life again.

You start to think about working on your own terms. You begin to value freedom over the next promotion. During this phase, you can also consider what work you have enjoyed and would like to continue. You can find a purpose for the second half of your life.

This is also the phase in which you're free to focus on shoring up the financial front from the carnage caused by kids and college costs. The good news is that you should be coming into your peak earning years at the same time. In an upcoming chapter, we'll discuss strategies to make the most of it.

One unique part of this season is that you have the chance to reimagine your work. While in college, we dream big, then fall into a career after graduation. Some of us end up loving it; many, however, end up seeing it as a means to an end, to provide for the family and build a retirement nest egg. Work/retirement isn't a binary choice. In fact, there are lots of personal and financial reasons to do both. As you'll see in the chapters ahead, if you're intentional, you can create a career plan unique to your needs and wants.

When I survey my clients and my podcast audience about what retirement means to them, the answer is consistent. Freedom and independence is what they want. Freedom to slow down and have time to do things they care about, and independence from the grinding workload of their career.

John says, "It's not that I want to stop working. I just want to stop working so hard. I want to have more time to spend with my Sarah and doing things I love."

This is the season to noodle on what you could do to get out of the daily grind and earn an income doing something you enjoy, something with more freedom and independence.

The good news here is that, unlike past generations, you have more opportunity than ever before. You have a wealth of experience, wisdom, and connections to call on, and the ability to "take those to market" has never been easier.

The objectives are to:

- Simplify your lifestyle.

- Rekindle interests and hobbies.

- Maximize your earnings in your career.

- Shore up your financial life.

- Begin reimagining what work you could do to give you more freedom and independence.

CREATE THE BEST OF BOTH WORLDS

Freedom: The absence of constraints. The ability or means.

Ahhh, the freedom phase; this is the sweet spot. Once you've simplified your lifestyle, shored up your finances, and discovered work you love, you can enter a phase with more freedom and independence.

This season isn't necessarily about money. Working is definitely a big help on the financial front, but it provides other great benefits: a sense of purpose and a source of intellectual, social, and physical engagement. In fact, doing work you love doesn't have to involve money. I've walked with clients who were busier than ever serving their church, family, or neighborhood.

My father-in-law was a lifelong worker at an auto company. He grew up in the coal region of western Virginia. His family worked in the coal mine, and he drove coal trucks during high school until joining the Army. It was his ticket out. He served honorably, and after he was discharged, he arrived in Pontiac, Michigan, without a high school diploma. During his career, which began at the bottom of the factory floor, he got his GED, took university courses, and worked his way up over thirty years to managing a division of an assembly plant. That's pretty impressive. Over that time, he built up a wealth of knowledge about every aspect of operating an efficient assembly plant.

When he retired in his early fifties, he immediately began to take mid-term assignments as an independent consultant for the same company. His experience was invaluable. He would work anywhere from three months to a year and earn enough to cover his family's basic lifestyle expenses. These assignments sent him to Mexico, Brazil, and other interesting places. He did this for over ten years. Why did he go back to work? Yeah, the money was nice, but it was also the challenge and excitement of still being able to solve the puzzle and have some free time.

Now in his seventies, he's become the go-to handyman for his entire neighborhood (and my house!). To this day, he remains engaged and continues to pursue his passion for fixing things.

Contrast this to my mother-in-law, Linda. When she retired after thirty years of moving up the corporate ladder at a human-resources company, she never "worked" again. Instead, she rekindled her passion for music and serving her church. Her freedom years are spent mentoring her daughters, showering affection upon her grandchildren, and performing in an award-winning handbell ensemble.

Then there's Mary. Mary liked to sew. For twenty years, she held an administrative position at an insurance company—not exciting work, but she liked the people and the hours were OK. When she was in her early fifties, her nephew came to her and asked for a favor. He knew she liked sewing, and he had a flag from an office building he managed that needed mending. She was happy to help and repaired it easily. This happened a few more times over the next year or so until the nephew came to her with a proposition. He worked for a property-management company that managed a lot of buildings in the Dallas–Fort Worth area. Each office building had anywhere from two to eight flags. He wondered if she'd be willing to take over repairs for more of the buildings. See, north Texas is a windy place, and flags need repair more often than one might think. Long story short, over time, Mary was able to leave her administrative position and actually make more money doing what she loved to do, with more independence and freedom than she'd ever had.

Oh, there are so many great examples!

Here's one last one. John and his wife are avid cyclists. I've had the chance to ride with them in cool places. They're amazingly interesting people and great organizers. Their plan is to organize bicycle tours during these freedom years. It will give them the chance to travel, cycle, and meet new people. Even if this small venture just pays for their travel, it's a huge win.

Whether it's consulting, sewing, playing handbells, being a barista, greeting customers at Walmart, being a handyman, driving for Uber, freelancing, teaching, tutoring, or being a board member or lawman, there are more opportunities than ever before to work—and do so on your own terms.

The value of working is immense. From a financial perspective, it will allow you to preserve or even grow your financial assets to help you have more financial security later in life. The early phase of retirement is typically the most risky. Big losses early on can be impossible to recover from. Working during the first ten years of retirement will allow you to take advantage of your position as a healthy, experienced, and wise contributor. This is the time to make hay. The key is discovering how to do this with more freedom and independence.

Finding work you love that gives you more control over your time can allow you to leave the career you may have fallen into earlier. Most of us wind up in our career through a series of choices early in life. Once we're out of college, the pressures of earning a living and supporting a family channel us into careers we may not have chosen in hindsight. Many times, we don't discover our true gifts and passions until later in life.

From a social perspective, finding work you love to do will help you build a new social network outside of your previous career. During our careers, our social life tends to revolve around our coworkers. It makes sense; these are the people you spend the most time with, given our overworked culture. In traditional retirement, you lose these people. Sure, at the retirement party, everyone says he or she will stay in touch, but as soon as you're on the outside, the things you have in common diminish. Finding part-time work in retirement helps you build a new network of friends.

You were meant to have purpose. It could be as simple as fishing or as big as starting a business. Your purpose is unique to you. Without it, something will fill the void. Finding work or something you enjoy that still offers the freedom to do the things you love keeps you from filling the void with potentially destructive behaviors. Remember the beer-and-peanuts guy? It could also be the shopaholic, golfaholic, or some other -aholic. Trust me, without purpose, you'll find something to pass the time.

YOUR PARENTS' RETIREMENT

Only after one to two years in the Simplify and Reimagine phase and ten to twenty years in the Best of Both Worlds phase does retirement start to look traditional. Working for income stops, and the retiree lives off assets and settles into a no-go phase of life. Reimagine retirement to include the first two phases; they're the best!

Remember the movie *Braveheart*? It tells the story of Sir William Wallace, the thirteenth-century Scotsman who rallied the Scots against English oppression. He organizes a haphazard army of commoners to battle the mighty English army. At the end of the movie, as his life is about to end by execution, surrounded by hundreds, he yells, "FREEEEDOMMMMM!"

Don't be like the film version of William Wallace. Don't yell "freedom!" at the very end of your life. You have the ability and the opportunity to reimagine your life in retirement now. If you choose, you can ignore the paint-by-numbers approach and create a masterpiece from which you may never want to retire.

CHAPTER SUMMARY

☐ **The Freedom Factor**—We value freedom more than retirement. Freedom to pursue our passions. Freedom over our time. Freedom to live life on our own terms.

☐ **Retirement Isn't a Date; It's a Relationship**—Most run from work rather than toward retirement.

☐ **Simplify and Reimagine (one to five years)**—Once the work of raising a family is done, start to simplify your life and begin to reimagine your life and work.

☐ **Best of Both Worlds (five to twenty years)**—In this season, you're doing work you love. You have control over your time and the freedom to pursue what's important to you.

☐ **Your Parents' Retirement (zero to twenty years)**—This is what we think of as traditional retirement, sitting on the park bench of life.

CHAPTER 4
EMBRACING UNCERTAINTY

"Making predictions is really hard,
especially about the future."

—CASEY STENGEL, BASEBALL MANAGER

Growing up, I thought doctors knew everything about health. Whatever they told you to do, you did, because they were super smart and they knew for certain what to do. No one told me this; it was just understood, sort of like always listening to your mother.

In my early twenties, this perception blew up for me when my mom battled and ultimately died of cancer. She had fought it once before and won. She was "cancer-free," and then she wasn't. She did everything the doctors told her to do, and none of it worked. Finally, she'd had enough and allowed the disease to run its course.

One lesson I learned from this is that, yes, doctors are super smart, but they don't know everything. They see a symptom, then run tests to give them clues, then guess on the diagnoses and possible treatment plans. The diagnoses and treatment plans can differ wildly from doctor to doctor. Some guesses are near certain, like for the mumps, but a lot of them are not. The point is, most of the time they don't know, regardless of how confident they seem.

It's like that even more so in managing your life and money. For the longest time in my career, I wanted to be like the doctor. I wanted to be the smartest one in the room. I wanted to figure it all out so I could be a rock star in my clients' eyes. I read every investment and planning book I could find. I studied for and passed almost every securities-license exam offered. I earned all but one of the most rigorous advanced certifications offered. I thought that if I accomplished all this, I could clearly choose the right path for clients to take. I could say with full confidence, "If you do this, this, and this, you *will* be OK."

It took me nearly twenty years to not just understand, but also truly accept the fact that you can't figure it all out. No one can. Even the super-smart people. At the end of the day, we're all just humans, muddling through. I know this isn't very comforting to read, but it's true; the sooner you accept it, the quicker you can stop chasing certainty and start having the right little conversations to manage your way through it.

UNCERTAINTY IS DISCONCERTING

Do you feel secure in this world? From a financial perspective, I know few who do. Even the very wealthy worry about whether they'll have enough, whether they'll be able to maintain the lifestyle they want. It's OK if you feel uncertain about your future. Join the club. You're a member along with 99.99999999999 percent of us.

As I've mentioned, a sixty-year-old in 2017 has a 50 percent chance of living past age ninety. Your generation (and quite possibly, you) will live almost a third of its adult life in "retirement." Imagine, thirty or forty years in retirement; that's a long time. I mean, a *really* long time. Think back over the last thirty years of your life. Think about the changes you've seen in:

- your family
- your health
- your career
- your finances
- your relationships
- the markets
- the economy
- the world!

I bet your life has had more twists and turns (good and bad) than you ever could have predicted.

I understand all this might not make you feel better. *You think, Who cares if everyone feels this way? I don't want to.* I hear you. I don't like it either, but it's what we get. Life is risk. You and I can't change it, no matter how smart we are. While you're alive, you'll never be without uncertainty—uncertainty about your health, your family, your career, your money, the country, the world, the universe. You'll never (can I repeat that?) NEVER be without uncertainty.

Uncertainty is disconcerting, so we look for answers. It's natural for us to want to eliminate as much uncertainty as we can, especially as we age. As we get older, we feel more vulnerable. We recognize we don't have the time or energy left to make up for big mistakes. I recall all the financial mistakes I made in my twenties and thirties—and there were some doozies: expensive cars, credit card debt, too big a house. Big mistakes. But I was young, and I had time and earning power on my side. I was able to earn my way out of the mistakes and recover. As we get older though, especially into our fifties, it gets harder to bounce back from financial mistakes, so we tend to worry more about the future.

Once we leave the workforce, our worry can increase. I've seen how not having a regular paycheck affects clients. Suddenly they feel at the mercy of things outside themselves: life events, interest rates, inflation, markets, risks. They've spent decades earning their own keep, saving, and building. That's very empowering. Then all of a sudden, in retirement, it stops. When bad financial things occur, it's nearly impossible to earn your way out of them. Even if you're highly skilled, your value to employers diminishes once you're out of the game. Your skills decay. Your professional network unravels. That's scary. I hear this sentiment expressed frequently from clients and listeners. They say it was unexpected and disconcerting.

DUCT TAPE VS. PROBLEM SOLVING

Ask my brother-in-law, and he'll tell you that duct tape is the solution to virtually any problem. Got a hole in your sock? Duct it! Cut your arm? Duct it! Kids won't be quiet? Duct them!! On my last visit, he showed me a website dedicated to how duct tape could fix anything.

It takes brain power and time to actually solve a problem. When we're feeling uncertain, it's easy to reach for the duct tape. Duct tape in this instance takes the form of most manufactured products. These quick "solutions" can give us an immediate, though fleeting, sense of comfort. Let's look at a few.

High cholesterol?

Duct tape: Take a pill.

Solving the problem: Change your diet and exercise.

Marriage problems?

Duct tape: Take a BIG vacation so you can have "quality time."

Solving the problem: Establish a weekly date night to discuss life and stay connected.

Retirement savings low?

Duct tape: Take advantage of trading systems that never fail, real estate with no money down, day trading, house flipping, etc.Solving the problem: Do the work to increase your income and control spending.

Worried about markets?

Duct tape: Buy a product like an annuity, hedge fund, etc.

Solving the problem: Find a sound investment process and follow it religiously to make lots of small smart decisions and/or find fun part-time work that brings joy and money to you.

Worried about running out of money?

Duct tape: Buy high-cost insurance products with income guarantees.

Solving the problem: Take control of your financial future by having the right conversations.

It's easy to grasp for solutions/products when we're worried about something, especially financial security and retirement. And guess what? There are thousands of companies spending billions of dollars on marketing and salespeople telling you they have the "solution." Buying one may take away the short-term discomfort, but it rarely solves the problem.

Over the years as a financial advisor, I saw the "you have a problem; we have a solution" cycle play out again and again. In the 1990s, when technology and Internet stocks were hot, everyone wanted them and virtually every new mutual fund had "Tech" or "Internet" in the name. When tech stocks crashed and investors clamored for safety, "principal-protected funds" were introduced to meet the demand. In the 2000s, it was variable annuities, then hedge funds, then indexed annuities, commodity funds, and infrastructure funds. Each worry was met by a new expensive, unproven product. There was a roll of duct tape to cover up any worry you had.

I not only saw these new products, I also sold them. During the tech-stock meltdown in the early 2000s, people had too many of these "great" investments going into the downturn, and as a result, their taste for investing soured. They wanted security. So did I and other advisors; we were afraid too. It's not fun disappointing clients. When the friendly investment-product representative visited and talked about the new principal-protected funds, it was like manna from Heaven. It was the solution (duct tape) to take away the immediate pain from us and our clients.

Postscript: Principal-protected funds sucked as investments. Markets became normal again, and they greatly underperformed. Similarly, after the Great Recession of 2007–2009 when the market tumbled, the sales of fixed annuities skyrocketed (duct tape). Advisors and investors again rushed into very conservative low-returning products just in time to miss all the returns of the recovering markets. The story repeats itself over and over.

So be warned: When you have a worry, there will be someone there to sell you a roll of duct tape. It will feel good in the moment, but ultimately, it won't solve the problem. If you want a chance to live with more freedom and retire successfully, you're going to have to take responsibility and control over your financial future. Embracing uncertainty is the first step. When we embrace uncertainty and learn how to manage despite it as our life unfolds, we take our power back.

SMART PEOPLE CAN'T PREDICT THE FUTURE

The movie *Zero Dark Thirty* tells the story of the search for Osama bin Laden. In one scene, the director of the CIA, played by James Gandolfini, is walking to the elevator with his assistant, Jeremy, after listening to a briefing from the lead analyst on her conclusions about Bin Laden's location.

As they're walking, the CIA director asks Jeremy, "What do you think of the girl?"

Jeremy replies, "I think she's f'ing smart."

The director stops, pauses, turns, and says, "We're all smart, Jeremy."

This scene stuck with me. There are lots of super-smart people in finance. Walk into any brokerage firm or turn on any financial channel, and you'll see them. They have impeccable credentials, impressive offices, fancy suits, and all the facts and figures at the tip of their tongue. These people are smart. And they're not alone. These smart people work in teams with other really smart people. They have the most sophisticated tools, analysts, strategists, economists, technicians, quants, traders, and researchers. They produce amazingly smart research reports and forecasts. They know smart things nobody else knows and can out-smart-talk us all. It's easy to agree with their "we're smart, serious people and you should listen to us" attitude.

I know. I was one of these smart people. Like them, I thought that if I just learned more, researched more, I'd figure it out.

Like doctors, most planners in the financial-advice industry want to do what's best for the client. They want to take the pain away and make everything all right. Patients and investors rely on answers given by super-smart people with super-strong convictions, wearing white coats or fancy suits. It sure seems like these smart people know what they're doing, so we listen. We give them our money and believe them when they tell us they have it under control.

But they don't.

Relying on "smart people" who say they can take away the uncertainty or predict what will be hot is a recipe for financial disaster—*your* financial disaster. Their smarts and confidence may be comforting in the short term, but you are betting your financial future on them being right.

I got an email from a podcast listener telling me that a friend, just a few years into retirement, was instructed by his advisor to cash out all of his investments because of the recent downturn in the market. Here was an advisor recommending an extreme, and frankly ill-advised, move (most extreme advice is precisely that). The listener's friend was inclined to follow the advice, because the markets are not his area of expertise. He was told something that made some sense to him: He should sell everything because he had just lost money, and it could get a lot worse. He's got to rely on his advisor, right? Yikes!

The fact that the advisor likely had no profit motive makes his recommendation all the more insidious. If he was a fee-only advisor, he didn't get commission on this extreme advice. He likely gave it because he believed his prediction of future events.

It seems a bit silly for me to list all the horrible failures of Wall Street here. Virtually every serious study has concluded that Wall Street gurus are no better at predicting markets, economies, and company performance than you or I. Wall Street is great at selling research and products, but it's not good at predicting the future. A recent Forbes headline declared, "It's Official! Gurus Can't Accurately Predict Markets." The article goes on to say, ". . . market experts accurately predicted market direction only 48 percent of the time." Among the gurus studied by CXO Advisory Group, LLC, Forbes said the best performing guru had a 68.2 percent grade while the worst performing one had a 21.7 percent grade. Rather cynically, but accurately, Forbes said, forecasting isn't about predicting the market; it's about marketing the prediction (Ferri 2013).

CBS News reported Jan Hatzius, the chief economist of Goldman Sachs, talking about the value of economic forecasts, "Nobody has a clue. It's hugely difficult to forecast the business cycle. Understanding an organism as complex as the economy is very hard." Larry Swedroe, director of Research for Buckingham Strategic Wealth, writes, "Accuracy isn't important to investors. Confident talking heads is what they seek. Investors want a clear crystal ball. They want to believe that there's someone out there who can protect them from bad things. Unfortunately, no such person exists" (Swedroe 2012).

It's true. No such person exists, no matter the size of his office or type of wood lining the walls. When we strive for predictability in an unpredictable world, we're betting our financial well-being on someone's ability to predict the future. I don't want to bet my life on someone else's ability to predict the future, especially when I know he or she can't. If I'm not going to attempt to shift the responsibility to someone else, I have to embrace uncertainty, come to terms with it, and figure out how to move forward.

Run from people like that advisor who told his client to cash out all his investments. Run from those with extreme thinking. In fact, run from anyone who bases his or her advice on predictions or forecasts.

You want somebody who is humble enough to realize that all of this is unknowable, and who gives you a process to manage getting through it. You don't want somebody who has all the answers, because there is no such thing as "all the answers."

YOU CAN'T PREDICT THE FUTURE EITHER

"What?!?" you exclaim. "Certainly I can trust myself when it comes to my life. I'm the captain of my ship! I control my own destiny!" True, you are the captain. You can set sail on a clear, sunny day and plot your course, but you are a small craft on a huge ocean. Some may question Mike Tyson's intellect, but he was dead-on with this observation: "Everyone has a plan 'til they get punched in the mouth." This may be mixing metaphors, but it gets the point across. If we're intentional, we can manage the rudder and steer, but the ocean of life can *and will* punch us in the mouth from time to time, pushing us far off course. Let's look at some examples.

Life's Sucker Punch

At the age of sixty-one, Mark and his wife, Rita, retired. They had worked feverishly for ten years to position themselves well, financially speaking. She worked as an international flight attendant for years and slowed down to two days a week. It was a great early-retirement job that gave them income, benefits, and the ability to fly for free. They were thrilled to finally be able to spend time together raising their animals on a small farm and visiting their grandchildren.

The first two years of retirement were wonderful. Mark became a gentleman farmer, raising chickens and goats. He reminded me of Oliver from the old TV series *Green Acres*. Rita loved the balance of flying and being able to visit all the grandchildren.

All was going according to plan until late one night in July. That night, around 11:30 p.m., Rita was driving home from the airport when she lost control of her car on a country road. No one knows why. Perhaps she swerved to avoid a dog or a deer. All we know is that she died that night.

No one could have predicted such a horrible event. They had done everything right. They had taken care of themselves. They'd owned cars with modern safety features, had always worn their seat belts, and had driven at safe speeds. This tragedy just happened.

Mark and Rita enjoyed two wonderful years, but that was only a very small piece of what they'd planned and worked for.

Lady Luck

Ethel grew up on her family's ranch, a few thousand acres in North Texas. For generations, her family raised cattle and farmed, though

Ethel never did. After college, she chose to live in the city, about fifty miles from the homestead. When her parents passed and she inherited the land, she leased it out to a local rancher. The lease payments provided a nice supplement to her income from her office-manager position, but it wasn't a life-changing amount.

Fifteen years after her parents passed, when Ethel was forty-eight, she received a letter from an oil and gas company. They believed there was natural gas under her ranch and asked to lease the rights to extract it. They offered her a lump sum payment of $15,000 for the rights. If they ever decided to drill, they'd share a percentage of whatever they found. Ethel agreed and used the upfront payment to embark on the European trip she had always dreamed of taking.

For two years, she heard nothing from the company and saw no activity when she visited her ranch. Then suddenly, she received a royalty check for $10,000! *There must be some mistake,* she thought. When she called to ask about it, they told her that a new technology called horizontal drilling had been developed that allowed them to extract the gas from a far-off well. A little while later, she was receiving monthly royalty checks of $50,000.

Just like no one could have predicted the tragedy Mark and Rita suffered, no one could have predicted the fortune thrust upon Ethel. Life just happens that way.

Investing Is Easy

In the late 1980s, Bill decided to retire. He was fifty-seven and had done well for himself. He managed his own investments and was a follower of famous investment manager Peter Lynch. Lynch managed the Fidelity Magellan Fund and has one of the greatest performance track records ever. The famous manager was convinced that the average investor could beat most professionals by investing in what he or she knew. Bill liked the simple philosophy and used it to manage his 401(k).

When Bill retired, he invested all of his assets into a portfolio of stocks based on Lynch's strategy. He stayed fully invested, selling just enough to pay for his living expenses each year, and did amazingly well. Fifteen years after retirement, not only had Bill supported his life in retirement, his assets had grown substantially. By the time the markets corrected in 2000, he was over seventy, collecting Social Security and financially fine. Although he didn't catch a hook to the mouth, as Mike Tyson suggested, Bill could have. Sometimes when you set sail, it's a perfect voyage. Bill's was because he had the winds of many years of positive stock returns at his back. Had he set sail when returns were poor early on, his voyage would have been much different . . . more like Phil's.

Investing Sucks

Phil had done everything right. He and his wife had met with a financial advisor in 1999, when their first child was four years old, to start saving for college and retirement. Their financial advisor helped map out a systematic investing plan where each month they would contribute to a college savings plan, 401(k), and taxable investment account. All told, each month they saved 22 percent of their income. The advisor showed them a chart illustrating how, over time, college would be paid for, and over even more time, they would be millionaires. Phil liked that. He also liked the idea that now he wouldn't have to worry and could use his raises to pay for his growing family.

One year after starting his investment plan, the markets crashed. Phil was nervous, but his advisor assured him that this was good. Because Phil's plan was systematic, he would be buying at cheaper prices. The advice proved true. The markets slowly recovered and their accounts grew. Then the Great Recession happened. As the markets fell, Phil grew more and more concerned, but his advisor assured him all would be OK. The firm's strategists felt the downturn would be short-lived.

Ten years into his investment scheme, Phil's account had barely grown. In fact, he had lost some money. His oldest child was now fourteen, and there wasn't close to enough money to pay for his college education, not to mention his little sister's. The markets continued to fall, and by the beginning of 2009, Phil had had enough. He got out. He rescued his full investment, but with no return over his ten-year trek. Subsequently, the markets rose again.

THE ONLY CERTAINTY IS UNCERTAINTY

It's impossible to know if you will experience no wind, strong winds, or a hurricane. It's best not to tempt fate and risk your family's financial future by blindly following smart people or being overconfident in your own abilities.

It is far better to embrace uncertainty and learn how to navigate your way through it as your life unfolds. Accepting uncertainty as fact will save you hours every day and days every year. By getting off the prediction train, you'll stop watching market forecasts, searching for gurus, being sold products, and second-guessing every decision you make.

Embracing uncertainty also makes you scam-proof. It makes you more immune to the siren songs we hear every day of, "Follow me. I have all the answers." It allows us to call bs when we hear radio commercials or go to a seminar led by an extremely well-dressed advisor proclaiming how smart he is and predicting what's going to happen.

REAL FREEDOM

Once we accept that the future is unknowable, really accept it, really embrace it, it frees us to begin the work of taking control of our life and directing it. This is important to me personally as well. I got into the finance business because I love finance. I wanted to be *that* market strategist, the infallible stock picker. Most people in my industry never let go of that desire, even with decades of documented history showing that they don't know what they're doing. When I finally accepted uncertainty as an advisor, which took much longer than it needed to, it freed me from the tyranny of CNBC, Fox Business News, and Bloomberg. I don't need to have my ear glued to the TV or spend all my free time reading market forecasts. I read a few here and there to be able to join the conversation with my clients, but they aren't the center point of my life. Most importantly, embracing uncertainty put front and center the choice to either flounder in the ocean alone or to build a framework to manage the uncertainty in my life and the lives of my clients.

Rather than trying to figure it all out, what we need is a process to get through the uncertainties, to stay the course in the rough ocean. That process hinges on having the right conversations to make adjustments as life unfolds, whether it's the markets, the economy, or your personal life.

CHAPTER SUMMARY

☐ **Uncertainty Is Disconcerting**—We crave certainty, especially in retirement. The drive to eliminate it can cause us to grasp for answers that aren't really there.

☐ **Duct Tape vs. Problem Solving**—There are plenty of people ready and willing to sell us a "solution" to our retirement worries. Like duct tape, these solutions are temporary fixes.

☐ **Smart People Can't Predict the Future**—Even with millions of dollars and thousands of hours of brain power spent analyzing it, the future is unknowable.

☐ **You Can't Predict the Future Either**—Although we hold the rudder directing our life, we are at the whim of fate.

☐ **Real Freedom**—Once you accept the future as unknowable, really accept it, really embrace it, you are free to begin the work of taking control of your life and directing it.

CHAPTER 5
DREAM BIG ABOUT YOUR RETIREMENT

"There is no passion to be found playing small—
in settling for a life that is less than the one
you are capable of living."

—NELSON MANDELA

How do you jump off the train barreling toward a retirement of bad choices? How do you redefine and rock your retirement? It all starts with changing how you think about planning for your future. It starts with imagining what the masterpiece of your life will look like when complete, in full vivid detail. Crumple up the paint-by-numbers canvas and start with a blank one, one big enough to hold your life in all its glory.

When we think about setting goals, it's easy to be conservative. The news outlets constantly tell us we are in a "retirement crisis." We should be "reasonable." Why should you expect your retirement to rock? "Lower your expectations for your life" is what they say, because their paint-by-numbers approach can't see any other picture. Their limited vision can crush your creativity and possibly your life.

When you sit down with a financial planner, or with your spouse, it's easy to stay within the lines and come up with something plausible and feasible. "Best to follow their advice," you say, "They're the experts." But in this case, being reasonable isn't a virtue; it's a vice. It can cause you to shortchange your life and the precious time you have with friends and family. There's nothing more tragic.

I'm giving you permission to paint outside the lines, permission to create a life that is your unique masterpiece. Permission to dream big about what your life could look like. Don't panic; we're just dreaming now. You're drawing in pencil. Nothing is decided; nothing is set in stone. Just take this journey with me and dream— with a few ground rules.

DON'T BE REASONABLE

I did a Google search for "retirement crisis" and found 22,800,000 results in less than half a second. When I searched "retirement dreams," Google gave me 713,000. That's 22,800,000 vs. 713,000!!! America's retirement crisis is a favorite topic for the financial industry and media. They say:

"Market returns won't be good enough."

"Your best has come and gone."

"Health-care costs will eat your lunch."

"You're going to live too long."

"Interest rates are too low."

"You're not saving enough."

"Inflation will be too high."

"You'll spend too much."

"The future isn't bright."

No wonder so many clients struggle to dream big about their life. They've come to believe pursuing a great life in retirement is unrealistic. The paint-by-numbers approach keeps them well within the lines. With their imagination stunted, they dream small and stick to whatever the calculator says they can get.

I say, don't sacrifice your masterpiece at the altar of "being reasonable." Please. *Please* don't be that person. Don't give up on creating your own unique masterpiece. Don't sacrifice your life. Don't sacrifice because you're worried about the future, or because you've been conditioned that just getting to retire is reward enough.

First, it won't remove the worry. Worry about the future is never going to go away. Trust me. I've seen it in action. No matter how much money you have or how frugal you are, you're going to worry.

Second, why, oh why, would you not create a masterpiece with your life? Why would you sacrifice the only life you have before you've explored all options for getting everything you can from your time here?

I can hear you. You're saying to yourself, "I can't believe Roger's trying to sell me that 'Shoot for the moon and if I miss, I'll be among the stars crap.' I can buy a poster for that, not read a book." Relax. I'm not. I am firmly grounded in the harsh realities about retirement.

Bluntly, some of us are screwed—financially speaking—when it comes to retirement. Some of us will be able to have all or most of what we want, and most of us will be somewhere in between.

What I'm saying is that before you resign yourself to a last third of life full of sacrifice, find out what might be possible. Find out what masterpiece you aspire to create. Find out how much you can squeeze out of life. The best way to do that is to start by thinking BIG.

Change Your Focus

Rather than focus on what you're running away from, focus on what you're running toward. Leaving your career just to make the pain go away is not a strategy for rocking retirement. Your boss may be horrible. The commute may be brutal. You may feel unappreciated. Your position may truly drain your soul. All of these things may be true, but don't let them be the sole driver of your decision to quit, retire, slow down, or start a business. Running *from* something keeps your focus on the past and present, not on the future, where it should be. When you retire to remove the pain, you wake up to discover you're lost. Remember the beer and peanuts guy from a few chapters ago? Like him. Stop focusing on what is and start dreaming up what your life's masterpiece *will be.*

Focusing on your future is the first phase of retirement and happens early on. Just as you're hitting the height of your career and right-sizing your lifestyle, spend time thinking, dreaming, about what your life could be—what your renaissance could look like. Focus on what you're running toward. This simple shift can empower and inspire you to define a vision for your life's work. Trust me, this isn't psychobabble. I've participated in these discussions with clients, and the transformation in mind-set is amazing. It empowers you to take control of your future.

Seth and Mary lived in Middle America for twenty-seven years. When we began to discuss life after full-time work, they painted the typical picture: stay in their home, take two trips each year, spend their time golfing, volunteering at the church, and loving on their kids and grandkids. A great retirement, no doubt, but definitely a paint-by-numbers one. As we talked, Seth and Mary began to reveal visions they'd had that each had only shared in passing with each other.

The impact of the mission trip Seth took in 2010 to Haiti to assist in the aftermath of their devastating earthquake had stayed with him. The people he helped were poor but working for a better life; they just needed a helping hand. As he began to draw outside the lines, he painted a vision of marshaling resources to help Haitians help themselves and coaching them along the way. As he talked, he leaned forward, sat upright, and his eyes came to life. He had no clue what the next step was in creating his masterpiece, but he had brushed the first stroke.

Mary's step outside the lines was less dramatic, but just as impactful. She revealed a secret desire to do stand-up comedy.

That's right; Mary wanted to be a comedienne. That was a first for me! And it made me laugh. She'd always had a quick wit, but I had never imagined this secret dream. Both Seth's and Mary's visions were completely possible but were only said aloud because they allowed themselves to dream.

It's important to point out that sharing a dream aloud doesn't make accomplishing it a requirement. To this date, Seth and Mary have not pursued the dreams we discussed that day. The conversation did help them, however, intentionally discuss the kind of life they wanted together. That's the point.

MAKE A S.W.A.G.

Sophisticated
Wildly
AWESOME
GUESS

As you go through the process of dreaming, you'll be tempted to jump back inside the lines and play it safe. Don't. Don't go calculating how much it will cost and all the reasons it's "silly." Your retirement is a blank canvas at this stage. You're dreaming up possible masterpieces. If you slide back inside the lines, you'll kill the process. Do you think that as Michelangelo began to envision his masterpiece *David*, he jumped right to calculating the number of hammer blows to his chisel and the strain on his body? In the face of that giant piece of marble, he probably would have concluded it was impossible, and that it was best to stay inside the lines and sculpt something less ambitious.

No matter how much research you do, you'll be wrong. The further out in time the item you're trying to calculate, the more wrong you'll be. Don't allow yourself to be bogged down by researching costs, adjusting for inflation, etc. It will kill your creative dreaming. Instead, at this stage, make a Sophisticated Wildly Awesome Guess (S.W.A.G.). You have my permission to just S.W.A.G. it. Make a guesstimate of the cost to achieve each dream. The point here isn't to build a detailed spreadsheet; it's to dream big. I understand this may be difficult for some of you engineer types. It's natural in our paint-by-numbers world to be practical. Our wanting detail is driven by the need for certainty, and we already know we can't have that. To some, this may seem immature. Only kids dream, right? If it helps, I promise that in a later step you'll be able to dial in some very detailed costs you can feel good about. Until then, just S.W.A.G. it.

IT'S NOT (JUST) ABOUT THE MONEY

"Money, money, money, money, MONEY. Some people got to have it. Some people really need it." I can just hear the O'Jays singing their hit song now. When you're dreaming up your ideal retirement, don't just focus on the money. I know plenty of folks rocking retirement who aren't "wealthy"—and I know some who are filthy rich who aren't.

Two fine men and friends, Bill Watkins and Robert Mallon of the Rusty Lion Academy, call it the curse of sequential living—the concept that we can only focus on one area of our life at a time. "I'll build my career, then be a great spouse." "I'll work like crazy, then take care of my body." "I'll enjoy today, then take care of the future." The idea that we invest heavily in one area of our lives while the rest waits seems to be part of the American work ethic. Watkins and Mallon suggest, and are living examples of, actually doing it all—living a balanced life. So when you're considering the future, don't place all your focus on the money, focus on all the components that make up a great life.

Health

Growing old doesn't have to mean slowing down; that's inside-the-lines thinking. As you grow older, how will you build and maintain a healthy mind, body, and spirit? Recall when we discussed how we'll live longer in "retirement" than any generation in history? Well, here's a secret: If you're unhealthy in mind, body, or spirit, you'll probably live almost as long as you would if you were healthy; it will just suck. You won't be able to do as much, you'll feel bad, and it will likely cost a lot more money.

How much strength of mind, body, and spirit do you think it took for Michelangelo to sculpt his *David* out of marble? Although he suffered from arthritis and kidney stones, he stayed active. In the *Journal of the Royal Society of Medicine,* researchers found that Michelangelo's continuous artistic work such as painting, hammering, and sculpting helped the artist maintain the use of his hands until his death (Laguipo 2016).

Part of rocking your retirement is being healthy. Regardless of your current health, there are things you can do to improve it. This may sound Pollyannaish, but it isn't. Nick Vujicic has no arms and no legs, yet he jumped outside the lines and is creating a masterpiece of his life. Through his organization, Life Without Limbs, he travels the world teaching by example that you can overcome any barrier life throws at you. Next time you let your health keep you inside the lines, watch a video of Nick.

Christopher Reeve was a handsome, physically strong man and movie star. Near the height of his career, while competing in an equestrian event, he was thrown from his horse. The accident destroyed vertebrae in his neck, separating his skull from his spine, and he was left paralyzed from the waist down. After a period of grief, he jumped outside the lines and became an activist and film director, and he returned to acting.

Consider Seth's vision of helping the people of Haiti. If he is overweight, out of shape, or depressed do you think he'll be able to create the masterpiece he envisions? Nope. He may have some impact, but it will likely be a faded version of what could have been a Technicolor life.

As you're dreaming up your ideal retirement, make sure you include ways to keep your mind, body, and spirit healthy.

> Go to rockretirementbook.com for an "Investing in Health" worksheet.

Relationships

I used to be a loner. As I've grown older, I see the value of connection. Friends like Eric, Darrell, John, Phil, Jamie, and others bring depth to my life that my younger self would never have understood. According to the American Public Health Association, healthy relationships lead to better lives (Johnson 2011).

The longer you live, the more likely your social network will naturally grow smaller. It's an all too common progression that leads to isolation. It goes like this: When you leave work, your colleagues drift away. As your children and grandchildren grow, they get busier and come around less often. Longtime friends are less able to travel, and the relationships fade away. Then your spouse passes, and the path to isolation is complete. It's sad, but it's a fact: If you are blessed with a long life, you could be the last man (or woman) standing. My grandmother was.

She passed away in 2015 at the age of ninety-five. She outlived all her sisters and brothers, two husbands, two daughters (one of them, my mother), one granddaughter, and virtually all her friends. She became isolated from all but a few of the people she cared for most in her life. Don't do that.

Be like Dan and Joanne Miller. They live life outside the lines. They're nearing seventy and have the richest social network I've ever seen (and I'm blessed to be part of it). They have young and old clamoring to come to their "sanctuary" to share a bit of life with them. How do they do it?

Joanne has nurtured her gifts as an artist, author, and speaker to connect with others. She has built an amazing shoe collection that brings people into her life, but it's not an Imelda Marcos shoe collection. Her shoes include (in her words):

- Wifey shoes

- Momma shoes

- Yia Yia and Nana shoes (She's also a grandmother.)

- Writer's shoes (She's written numerous books.)

- Artist's shoes (She's had art shows and has sold many pieces.)

- Teacher's shoes (She hosts a weekly art class open to beginners and the accomplished.)

- Connector's shoes ("I believe we all have a need for connection and no one I meet is simply random.")

Dan doesn't just live outside the lines; his life runs off the canvas, onto the floor, out the door, and around the world. Like Joanne, he does many impressive things. He writes books, hosts a podcast, teaches, and creates. He did one thing that anyone can do: He created a small group that meets regularly to connect, encourage, help, and challenge each other. He calls it the 48-Days Mastermind. It includes men and women of all ages. They meet each week via video call to discuss predetermined topics that focus on creating a rich life. A few times a year he hosts a retreat where we (I'm a member) meet for two days and deep dive into a particular area together.

Your canvas doesn't have to be painted like Joanne's or Dan's. Perhaps living outside the lines is mentoring via Junior Achievement, joining a book club, volunteering at the arts center, or attending weekly meetings at the local Waffle House. The canvas is blank and open to your wildest imagination.

Go to rockretirementbook.com for an "Investing in Relationships" worksheet.

Purpose

Does all purpose in your life evaporate when you retire? It shouldn't, but if you plan by numbers, it could. When you dream big about your retirement, cast a vision for what will be your purpose. Sketch out an image of what you'll get excited about.

Purpose can be an intimidating word. It conjures up images of conquering a mountain or of toiling toward some mammoth objective. And it *can* mean that. My friends Bill Watkins and Robert Mallon started Rusty Lion Academy in their late fifties with a goal to help one million younger men live better lives. That's a BIG purpose. Yours doesn't have to be. Yours could be as simple as deepening your relationship with your spouse or learning to garden. It can be anything you want. The point is to consider it and be intentional about nurturing it.

Why is this so important? Think back over your life. When have you *not* had purpose? In school, you had purpose: academics and/ or athletics. As an adult, your purpose was to build a career and/or a family. Outside of work and family, you've had passions like music, reading, crafting, etc. Volunteering, mentoring, woodworking, learning, singing in a choir, gardening, loving on the grandkids are all healthy examples. Unhealthy ones are shopping (this is a big one), drinking, overeating, shouting at the TV, etc. Without purpose, we begin to slowly fade. As you dream up your masterpiece, make sure to factor in something that brings purpose and meaning to each day.

USE A BIG ERASER

Remember when you were in school and the teacher always wanted you to write in pencil—a No. 2 pencil, to be exact. When you made a mistake, you could erase it, fix it, and move on. Dreaming big about your life is the same. The process is what's important, not "getting it right." When you sit down to dream up your ideal life, don't use a permanent marker; use an old, reliable No. 2 pencil . . . with a BIG eraser.

You're going to reimagine your ideal life many times as you age, and you may change your mind each time. That's OK; in fact, it's expected. Each year your life unfolds, you're going to become a whole new version of yourself. I joke that I've been married to five different women and my wife has been married to six different men, even though we were married right out of college and are, as of this writing, celebrating twenty-six years together. I'm not the same man I was ten years ago, and I won't be the same man ten years from now. My priorities, concerns, and dreams are different than they were five years ago, and very, very different than they were ten years ago. So relax, let go, and ask yourself, *If I could have it all, what would that be?*

THE SPAGHETTI THEORY OF RETIREMENT

PASTA + SAUCE + SPICE = GREAT LIFE!

To design the financial side of your retirement masterpiece, we're going into the kitchen. Cooking is art. To design your masterpiece, let's use spaghetti. Building your ideal retirement is like making a dish of spaghetti; really, it is!

Spaghetti consists of three elements: pasta (the base), sauce (the flavor), and seasoning (the spice). Your retirement will be made the same way. You're not going to do it like some fancy chef with a big white hat in a high-end kitchen. You're going to dream up your ideal retirement like an Italian mother makes spaghetti, singing away in a messy kitchen, adding a little of this, a pinch of that, a smidgen of spice, and a whole lotta love. Don't believe me? Read on.

Your Lifestyle Needs: The Pasta

If you were fired today, how much would you need each month to cover your expenses? I'm talking about basics like housing, utilities, groceries, medical bills, debt payments, insurance, etc. Would it be $6,000, $10,000, $20,000? This is the best place to start. You may even want to spend MORE in retirement then you do now. That's fine. What would it be? The monthly amount will be different for everyone. Some people love a bargain-store pasta, while others crave fancy pasta, and some like to make it from scratch—to each his own. It's your dream; it can be whatever you want, so dream it up.

I've found very few people have a good handle on what their basic lifestyle expenses are. Most think they do, but when they dig into the numbers, they're often surprised. It's OK to dream big and S.W.A.G. this amount at this stage, but the sooner you dial in this number, the better. It includes things like:

- Housing
- Utilities

- Health care

- Groceries

- Transportation

- Basic entertainment

- Clothing

- Insurance

- Taxes

If you're not careful, these basic lifestyle expenses can overpower your masterpiece. Have you ever eaten spaghetti with way too much pasta? It's pretty bland.

Your Wants: The Sauce

Pasta (basic lifestyle expenses) is a great start, but it's a bit boring don't you think? I bet you want a bit of flavor in your masterpiece, right? Like sauce adds flavor to a plate of spaghetti, your wants add flavor to your life. Use the tips below and start brainstorming the flavor you want in your life. What kind of vacations do you want to take? How often? What's the S.W.A.G. for it? Remember, this is dream setting, not goal setting. Don't use a measuring cup; if it's important to you, put it in the pot!!! How about:

- Vacation homes

- Destination vacations (paying for the whole family)

- Starting a business

- Starting a charity

- Learning a new skill

- Random acts of kindness to those in need

- Hitting the open road in an RV for a year

- Social clubs, golf clubs, tennis clubs, glee clubs, etc.

- Moving to a new state or country

- Living in a tiny home

- Expanding a current home

- Serving your church

- Running marathons

- Sailing seas

- Living for extended periods in exciting places

Your wants may be simple or complex. It's your dream. I've worked with plenty of clients whose ideal life would seem dull to others. *It's your masterpiece.* You're building it for you to enjoy, no one else. Don't feel like a stick in the mud if nothing on the list above stirs your soul. Don't feel greedy if the list above seems bland. Some people like spicy spaghetti; some don't. It's all cool.

Dreams: Here Comes the Spice Rack

You've got the right portion of pasta and you've chosen the sauce you love; now let's bring on the spices! This is where you put anything your heart desires. Perhaps you feel you've already asked for enough. This is often the case in our paint-by-numbers world.

You're not reheating a frozen dinner; you're an Italian-mama artist in the kitchen. Don't be afraid. *Put it in there.* This is *your life* you're creating; don't shortchange yourself. We'll have plenty of time to be reasonable later. Here are some dreams I've seen:

- Annual gifting to people you care about
- Annual gifting to an organization you care deeply about
- Leaving an inheritance
- Starting a foundation
- Multigenerational planning
- World travel
- Paying college costs for kids in need
- Paying for grandkids' education
- Paying off your children's mortgage

Go to rockretirementbook.com for a "Lifestyle Design" worksheet you can use to dream up your masterpiece.

Three Quick Cooking Tips

First, it's important to separate your ideal retirement into lifestyle needs, wants, and dreams. Don't blend them all together. Later on, when you start to prioritize what you really want, it'll be easier to separate priorities from dreams.

Second, don't worry if you're ideal isn't fancy, relative to that of others. Many aren't. It's not about spending or "living large." This is about creating a life *you* value. Do stretch yourself however. Rather than think in terms of things, think about experiences. What experiences would you like to create for yourself and those you love?

Third, if you're married, do this together. Simon and Garfunkel, Lennon and McCartney, Sonny and Cher, Hall and Oates—they were all better together. If you're married, make sure you create your masterpiece together. Have this talk, especially *this* talk, together. Your retirement masterpiece needs all four hands at work. No assuming you know what your partner wants; you know what they say about assumptions, right?

It's incredibly important that the two of you share the same vision for your life. Although when you married, you became one, you're still separate people. Your artistic vision may be different. Collaborating on the vision for your life can be a great conversation.

One key is to just listen . . . not judge. His or her vision is important, even if you don't share it. Listen to each other's vision, and put them both on paper. Once you've done that, you can begin to have open conversations to find a shared vision you can work toward.

Right now, my vision is to sell our house and move to a condo in downtown Fort Worth. I can see it in my mind's eye, and I like it. Ask my wife, and she'll tell you her vision is to continue to enjoy our home. It's actually become a bit of a joke with us. What will we do? We're not sure yet, but we're talking about it. We're exploring how to unify our visions for the future. Our current shared vision is to keep the home and explore the country by renting condos for three to six months a year.

Once you've created your shared vision, you're not done. Hey, it's marriage; you're never done, right? The two of you will need to schedule little conversations to review, confirm, and/or adjust your shared vision. In a later chapter, I'll show you how to do so.

Common Blockages

There are some very common hurdles in this process that I see over and over again. One common and unfortunate scenario is that discussions never take place between partners, and as soon as the kids leave the house, one of the partners announces, "I want out," much to the surprise of the other. Or people make their plans for retirement when they're younger, and once they get there, they look around and realize that they are different people now than the ones who planned that retirement. They think to themselves, *Wait, I wanted this?*

A classic disconnect in the failure to dream big is when partners decide that they're going to retire in their current house and never move. They agree to this plan together, and they (and their financial advisor) make their action plans and design their financial lives around it. In the meantime, grandchildren have arrived out of state, and one of the spouses starts thinking, "When I retire, I want to be near those grandbabies." But either that spouse never articulates this to his/her partner, or the partner doesn't actually hear it when he/she does. Suddenly, retirement is near, and now the plan is in trouble. Everything's blown up because one of their retirement goals changed with no communication about it or preparation in their financial plan.

Discussing your hopes and dreams with your partner is more than important; it's critical. I often use the analogy of a couple walking down a football field. They start together headed toward the far end zone of "our retirement." Along the way, one (or both) of the partners starts changing internally and begins walking a path that veers off from the spouse's, but both of them keep walking, not noticing their paths are not the same. By the time they get five yards from the end zone, the couple suddenly realizes they're miles apart from getting into that end zone together.

One more common scenario: One of the partners is actually embarrassed by his/her dreams and doesn't want to tell his/her spouse or financial advisor. Maybe it's something like being a comedian. Communication about aspirations and dreams can be scary, so it's important to create and maintain an accepting place for both partners to be able to communicate freely and without fear of ridicule or incredulity. Be open to hearing your partner's dreams, and be brave enough to admit yours.

HE WHO DIES WITH THE MOST MONEY LOSES

When you create your retirement masterpieces, know that while the biggest fear of most people is running out of money, more people die with *too much* money. The real cost of dying with too much money is foregone experiences with your spouse or with your family. Would it be better to leave a hundred thousand dollars to each kid or to use that a hundred thousand dollars to take everybody on a Disney cruise, including the grandkids, so you can create experiences and memories with the family? Connection or a cold check after you're gone? Dying with too much money, unless that's your intent, robs you and your loved ones of the masterpiece of life. So dream BIG!

CHAPTER SUMMARY

☐ **Don't Be Reasonable**—The first step in your journey is to imagine your ideal life. There will be time for being reasonable later in the process. Right now, *think big.*

☐ **S.W.A.G. It**—S.W.A.G. is a wildly awesome guess on the price tag for your dreams. At this stage, don't get bogged down in the details. There will be time for that later.

☐ **It's Not (Just) about the Money**—Money is an important, but not critical, factor in having a great retirement. Health, relationships, and purpose matter more. Don't ignore them.

☐ **Use a Big Eraser**—Your masterpiece will be an ever-changing work of art. As your life unfolds, your priorities and needs will change.

☐ **The Spaghetti Theory of Retirement**—Divide your financial needs between lifestyle needs, wants, and dreams.

CHAPTER 6
THE CASH FLOW EQUATION

"Happiness is positive cash flow."

—FRED ADLER, AUTHOR

With your retirement masterpiece clear in your mind's eye, it's time to dig into the important financial conversations to work to make it a reality. Cash flow is the lifeblood of your financial life, like paint is to a painter. If the paint stops flowing, the artist's masterpiece will be left unfinished. A bummer, but life will go on. On the other hand, if cash flow dries up while you're creating your masterpiece, you could go broke—and that is much worse. Best to apply some artistic (read: financial) discipline to assure this doesn't happen.

"OK, I can hear you, but I'm the artist of my life. Artists are free spirits. We can't be contained by artistic discipline. We must *live!!*"

In financial terms, that sentiment breaks down to, "OK, I hear you, but I have so many things I want to do. I want to enjoy today. I can't be contained by financial discipline. I must spend!"

Or maybe you already have financial discipline. In fact, if you're reading this book, you likely do. Even so, if you're going to thrive in your life outside the lines, it's important you know how to live inside the lines first—to understand the rules of the masters so you know which ones you can safely break. Let's start by reviewing the basic "inside the lines" stuff, and then move on to "outside the lines" strategies to help you thrive in retirement.

When I think of the concept of mastering the basics, the movie *The Karate Kid* comes to mind. In it, young Daniel, having just moved to a new neighborhood, gets bullied by some karate-wise locals. In the midst of the altercation, the mysterious Mr. Miyagi shows up and saves Daniel with *his* own masterful karate skills. Intrigued, young Daniel seeks out the wise old Mr. Miyagi to learn karate to defend himself. When Daniel shows up the first day of training, he's ready to get into the cool stuff. Instead, Mr. Miyagi hands him a soapy sponge and says "First wash all car. Wax on, right hand. Wax off, left hand. Wax on, wax off. Breathe in through nose, out the mouth. Wax on, wax off. Don't forget to breathe, very important." Daniel later learns that "wax on, wax off" wasn't just forced labor. It was teaching him basic karate techniques he could build upon.

Before we delve into the mysterious crane technique Daniel used at the end of the movie to win the day, let's learn to wax on, wax off. "Wax on" is identifying and organizing your sources of income. "Wax off" is monitoring and controlling spending. I know you want to jump right to the good stuff, but "Wax on, wax off. Wax on, wax off. Don't forget to breathe, very important!"

INCOME – SPENDING = $WEALTH CREATION
(wax on)   (wax off)

WAX ON

Your income today and tomorrow is your source to build wealth to help you create your masterpiece. Your first step is to identify, quantify, and track all your current sources of income. Income is the lifeblood of any business or household. It's what you'll use to live on (obviously) and build supplies, or wealth, for your future.

You need to know how much and what kind of paint you have now and how much you can expect in the future. Don't take this basic step, and you'll be like many I've encountered who are overflowing with paint (income), but let it spill all over the place as they slop it around and let it seep through the cracks in the floor. Don't be that guy or gal.

Let's start with current sources. You'll list things like:

- Income from work

- Bonuses

- Executive compensation such as stock options, restricted stock, performance units, deferred compensation, etc.

- Rental income

- Royalty income

- Business distributions

- Alimony

- Current pensions

- Gifts from family

- Lottery winnings, etc.

Virtually anything that is a current or normal inflow of money into the household should be listed.

Next, identify income sources you're counting on during retirement or extraordinary inflows in the future. These may be all of the above categories, plus:

- Social Security

- Pensions

- Inheritances

- Proceeds from deferred-compensation plans

- Part-time income

- Sale of assets such as a home, business, or other substantial asset

Use the "Income Impact" worksheet found at rockretirementbook.com to list how you earn income.

"Wax on" = Identify it, quantify it and track it. Don't forget to breathe. Very important.

WAX OFF

"Wax off" is managing spending. You can have all the paint or income in the world, but if you waste it, you'll never build wealth. You'll never have the supply of paint to create your masterpiece.

In my career, I've worked with plenty of people who've mastered "wax on" (earning income), but totally screwed up "wax off" (controlling spending). I once worked with a lady who earned over $1 million a year for over a decade and had almost nothing to show for it. All that paint she acquired seeped through the cracks in the form of houses, Bentleys, and travel. I crossed paths briefly with a billionaire. He needed help leveraging his assets for cash to pay his tax bill. The guy was worth over a billion dollars, and he didn't have the cash to pay taxes! I learned that ten years later, he lost it all.

Don't let this happen to you. Learn and/or refine the basics. Learn to wax off. To do this, we've gotta talk about the "B word."

The "B Word"

Wait, don't close the book!! We're not going to spend much time on the "B word," I promise, but a personal finance book wouldn't be complete without mentioning it; it's like a requirement or something. I'd be put in the advisor stockade and my colleagues would hurl spreadsheets at me if I failed to cite this. So let's just get this out of the way, then we'll move on to exciting stuff.

Budget . . . there, I said it. I just Googled "budget" and got 777,000,000 results in a half a second (isn't Google great?). Whenever we talk about managing cash flow, 99 percent of the discussion is around the "B word": how to set one up, which tool is best, how to track and categorize each penny you spend. You're relegated to a part-time bookkeeper so you can keep track and reconcile each teeny-weeny penny you spend.

The personal finance crowd *loves* to talk about budgets, yet according to financial guru Dave Ramsey, 68 percent of American adults still don't have a budget. Why? I have my own personal theory—though mind you, it's not very scientific. In fact, I have no data at all to back it up, just my own personal experience. Here's my theory—just taking a shot in the dark here.

MOST PEOPLE HATE TO BUDGET.

Most people don't keep a personal budget because keeping a budget is like having a gigantic leech on your face literally sucking the life force from your body. Who wants that? Not I. If you're part of the 68 percent who don't keep a budget, then probably not you either. OK . . . sorry. I get very worked up about this budget thing. That's how much I dislike it.

Budgets work for some.

I have many friends and clients who keep very detailed budgets and have done so for years. Some of their budgeting spreadsheets are truly works of art. They love the detail and find the process of recording, categorizing, and forecasting each transaction very enjoyable and productive. They feel empowered by managing and manipulating the data to project what the future might look like. In fact, I'll admit, I love working with people like this. It is very helpful that they're so organized in their spending. May God bless these people. I'm just not one of them. If you are, God bless you too. Have at it.

If you are like me and not one of these blessed people (and I do envy them), the key is to find a system that works for you. Given that there are over 777,000,000 sources on how to budget and 68 percent of people still don't do it, I don't think me becoming source 777,000,001 is going to change your mind. "Oh, since *Roger* said to budget, I'll do it." Nope. I don't think you're going to say that, so we had better find an easier way.

The goal of "wax off" is to control spending so we have more money coming in than going out. This is called "free cash flow" in business. Free cash flow is what builds wealth. The more free cash flow you create, the more cool choices you have on what to do with it. Imagine being an artist with a pallet containing *all* the colors in every texture imaginable. What kind of retirement masterpiece could you create? That's why this is so important. If you hate budgeting like I do but still want to build your supply of paint or wealth, then let me share how I've done it.

Roger's Super-Simple Anti-Budget Budget

STEP 1

Nickname your current checking account "Spending Account." This is the account from which you'll spend money. You'll pay all your family's expenses from this account. Most likely, this is your personal or joint checking account.

STEP 2

Create a separate account, nicknamed "Income Account." You'll use this account to receive any and all income. Paychecks, expense checks, bonuses, incentives, gifts from Aunt Betty, etc., go in here. Any money you get goes into this account. I've found it best to have this account at a different bank than the spending account. It helps keep it out of sight when you check your spending account balance throughout the month. You'll see why that's important in Step 4.

STEP 3

Determine your "Baseline Monthly Burn." This is the one step that will take a bit of effort. Our goal here is to set a monthly spending amount for the household. If you'd like, you can just S.W.A.G. it and set an initial amount. Why just S.W.A.G. it? Because you'll end up adjusting it as you implement the system. To S.W.A.G. it, look at the last four months of spending, take the average, and then make adjustments in the first few months. If you S.W.A.G. it, go to Step 4. If you'd prefer a more accurate estimate, continue on here in Step 3.

Print or download your last three monthly bank statements and list your fixed monthly expenses. These are the items you know you'll have to pay every month. Some of them, like the phone bill, won't be same each month, and that's OK. Use the highest amount of the last three months. Examples include:

- Mortgage

- 2nd mortgage
- Monthly savings/investments
- Real estate tax reserve
- Home insurance reserve
- Auto insurance
- Health insurance premium
- Life insurance premium
- Auto loans(s)
- Student loan(s)
- Club dues
- School tuition
- Consumer debt payment(s)
- Allowance (kids)
- Phone bill(s)
- Cable/Internet

STEP 4

Once you've determined your baseline monthly expenses, you're ready to start the system. Each month on a date that works for you, (it's the first for me) transfer your "Baseline Monthly Burn" amount from your "Income Account" to your "Spending Account." This is the money you have to spend for the month. It's your new paycheck.

As the month progresses, you'll see the balance dwindle. By the last week of the month, when you check your balance, you'll be sensitive to the less than comfortable cash cushion. Good. That's what you want. Just like water flows to the lowest point, our spending flows to the lowest balance. When we keep all your money within easy reach, it gets gobbled up. Segregating your excess income into an account you don't see each time you log into your bank makes you think of it differently.

What happens if, in week three, you notice you're on track to overshoot your monthly amount? Maybe you had extra expenses hit during the month like car or home repairs. No worries. You can transfer over enough to get you through the month. Before you do though, have a conversation (with yourself or your partner) about why it happened and jointly agree on the amount to transfer. Often clients will keep their Income Account with me so they have to have a conversation with me before accessing excess income. Now that's a tough accountability partner.

If, after three months, you find you're always going over your Baseline Monthly Burn amount, review why and adjust it. The key is to find an amount that lets you live, but still captures excess income.

The advantages of Roger's Super-Simple Anti-Budget Budget are:

1. You get some life back. You get to quit your part-time position as the bookkeeper of your financial life. No more frustrating nights tracking, categorizing, and—*ugh*—reconciling account balances.

2. You'll have better conversations about money. Generally each spouse does the spending for certain categories. In

a normal budget, if you go over in a category, the question is, "Honey, why did you spend so much in X category?" Regardless of how sweetly you say it, it will be taken as an attack. With this system, you can work on keeping within the monthly target as a team.

3. You keep the flexibility to identify hot spots. Gone are the days of shuffling through reams of paper to figure out what's happening. If you're consistently spending over your target, you can easily download your transactions to a spreadsheet and manipulate the data to find the issue.

4. You'll forestall lifestyle creep. I don't know about you, but I'm a big creeper. Wait, that sounds, . . . well, creepy. Lifestyle creep is like a thief in the night. Without the system, when you get a raise, bonus, or check from Aunt Betsy, it gets deposited into your checking account and is spent. Before you know it, you're driving a nicer car and living in a nicer home with nicer things. See how that happens. Roger's Super-Simple Anti-Budget Budget helps prevent that. As your income grows, it never gets put into the easily available bucket.

5. You're still in control of all the cash.

6. Last, and most importantly, you capture your excess income.

To get started, use the "I Hate to Budget" worksheet found at rockretirementbook.com.

"Wax off" = Your money is going somewhere and you need to find it, plug it, and gain control of your cash flow. Don't forget to breathe. Very important.

THE INCOME IMPACT

There is a group of people I see who've mastered the spending side, but who have little money because they can't create enough income. What if you're one of the people whose income is just paying the bills? Even though you're saving, it's not enough to move the dial on creating a retirement masterpiece. What then?

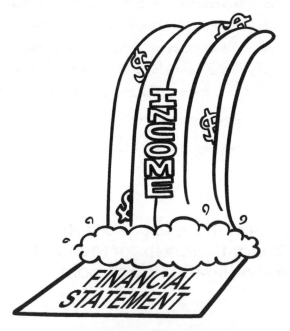

Inside-the-box thinking will tell you to focus on budgeting. It will say, *Spend less so you can save for your future.* That can help... as far as it will go. But like we said before, it's probably not going to move the dial much. As my friend, Paula Pant of *Afford Anything* says, "There is only so much frugaling you can do." I've sat with countless clients and reviewed their spending. When we look at the total, they say things like, "I can't believe we spend so much! There must be places we can cut." But when we review each category: groceries, utilities, phone bill, cable bill, travel, etc., rarely does one thing stand out as crazily excessive. Sure, maybe you could cut the cable bill or pack your own lunch more, but will it really move the dial in your financial life? It may help, but it's not a game changer.

Now I'm *not* telling you not to control your spending. What I'm saying is, this isn't where the big opportunity lies. We spend so much time trying to be frugal, we forget about the *huge* lever sitting right in front of us, just waiting for us to pull it: our income. Saving $300 per month by taking your lunch to work is great. Finding a way to increase your income by 20 percent or more is a game changer. If you make $80,000, a 20 percent increase is a sweet $16,000! That's a big lever. You just need to start thinking outside the lines to get it.

In business, they say rising revenue solves most problems. The same is true in your life; rising income solves most financial problems. Yet you find few people, especially those over fifty, tinkering with the income side of the cash flow equation. This, my dear friend, is powerful. Focus on how to increase your income, not just now, but in retirement as well.

Step 1: Identify Opportunities

The best way to build wealth and work toward your retirement masterpiece is the old-fashioned way: by increasing your income. Why is this so important? Wealth isn't created in the ways the media highlight. It's not inheriting a million dollars, playing the stock market, or winning the lottery. It doesn't matter if you're a Rockefeller or a plain Jane from Indiana. If you create more cash than you spend, and use that cash productively, wealth is created. This may appear simplistic, but it's very important. This is how you create wealth for yourself now and during retirement, and the sooner you look at your opportunities, the better. You are the driving force of your wealth creation, and income is how you do it.

Where do opportunities lie for you? In all honesty, the opportunities are various and plentiful. Here are two areas to start looking.

Your Skills

Investing in yourself is one of the best investments you can make. Worried about the economy, outsourcing, cutbacks, or reorganizations? One of the best defenses is to be so highly skilled and crucial, they can't do without you. Want a promotion in your current company or a job offer from a competitor? Acquire the skills that will make you a shoo-in for it. What exactly should you do? Heck, I don't know. I have no clue what your profession is. What I do know, however, is that virtually every profession has ways to earn advanced certifications.

Just look at me: Roger Whitney, CFP®, CIMA®, CPWA®, AIF®. Friends often joke that I have more letters after my name than *in* my name. Once I found my calling, I pursued the top certifications within my industry. I was careful to choose the most respected ones (there are *lots* of useless ones). Once I earned them, I jumped at the chance to teach others. When the opportunity was presented to teach Module 4 of the Certified Financial Planning Certificate program, "Retirement Planning and Employee Benefits," I said yes. I taught it for three years at the University of Texas at Arlington. The pay was small; the time investment was not. The education I received from teaching was priceless.

How do I measure the return on investment for these credentials? Hmmmm. It's difficult sometimes to put a hard dollar amount on education. Did my certifications tip the scales in my favor in winning a client? Did they help prepare me to write this (hopefully) best-selling book? Definitely. Did they prepare me to shine and add serious value for my clients? Absolutely. Evaluate your profession. What skills can you acquire to elevate your artistry in what you do?

A quick final note here about developing your skills: Our parents learned one skill that carried them throughout their working life. If you learned to be a phone operator or got a job in a factory, there was an implicit contract that you could continue with, and possibly advance within, the same company for your whole career. That's not the case today.

Today, the original job you acquired skills for could easily become obsolete. When is the last time you dialed zero and talked to an operator? Possibly never. Know anyone who worked in a factory or as a corporate manager, who has been laid off? Most certainly. Unlike our parents, the skills we learn can decay quickly.

It's a scary thought, I know. I've worked with clients in their mid-forties or mid-fifties who found themselves out of work with no attractive options in their field and no new field to pivot to. Simply doing good work won't cut it anymore.

While scary, this reality is also an opportunity. You are much more than your career. In fact, it's quite possible that now that you're in your forties or fifties, you realize your true gifts lie elsewhere. It's common to fall into a career out of college and not realize until years later that it's not your true calling. By the time you do realize it, you've got a spouse, a few kiddos, and a mortgage to pay.

So while you're identifying the skills to help get you ahead in your career, make sure you identify and nurture your natural talents. They may be the key to thriving later in life.

> Use the "Skill Development" worksheet found at rockretirementbook.com.

Your Network

It's not *what* you know, but *whom* you know. It sounds a bit crass, but it's true. Maybe a better mantra is "Friends do business with friends." We just naturally feel better doing business with people we know, like, and trust. You can be the best skilled carpenter within one hundred miles, but if no one knows you, you'll starve. You could be a perfect fit for an open position at a company in your field, but if they don't know, like, and/or trust you, you may never be considered. If there were *one* thing I'd go back and tell my twenty-year-old self, it would be to intentionally build and nurture my personal and professional network.

My friend Marc Miller of Career Pivot coaching says, "Relationships are key to every facet of managing your current or encore career. Investing time to cultivate new and reinvigorate old relationships is invaluable. Your next job, whether full- or part-time, will most likely come through a relationship. This is an invaluable investment that will pay for itself over and over again."

How well are you known in the company you work for? Are you considered an "A" player or a cog in the machine? It's the "A" players who get tapped when a new opportunity opens up or a project appears that has to get done. Doing your work isn't enough.

If you're like me, "networking" conjures images of those local events where everyone walks around shaking hands, looking to hand out business cards and give their "elevator pitch." Artificial networking is like predators roaming around looking for prey that they can sell something to; it's all about the transaction. It may work for some, but not for me. I'm talking about making friends, about being intentional, about personally connecting and nurturing a professional relationship. Rather than the hunt-and-kill mentality of traditional networking, this is more about growing an orchard. It's a long-term investment in relationships that may bear fruit years into the future.

A good friend of mine has taken this concept to the extreme. For years, he has slowly built a massive network of friends across the world—and I mean massive. He keeps a database in which he tracks personal tidbits about each person and important dates. His network is so large that he personally calls three to five people per day to wish them a happy birthday (and emails even more). He travels a lot for work, and before each trip, he researches who he can reconnect with in the area. Be it Paris, New York, Baton

Rouge, or Punxsutawney, he's likely to know someone with whom to reconnect. If he connects with you, he documents it with a picture and writes of the experience on his personal blog. The key is, he's authentic. Although he is now a high-powered CEO, he connects with anyone he admires. CEOs, COOs, CIOs, Marriott front-desk clerks, Uber drivers, or shoe shiners, it doesn't matter. If he likes you, he stays in touch.

I asked him how this has benefited him in business over the years. He said he's helped others find jobs, hired great people, been offered opportunities, and closed multimillion-dollar deals as a result of his network.

"Good things happen when you stay in touch with good people," he said. "You get the chance from time to time to help others, and they get the chance to help you."

Do you need to be as fanatical about networking as this man? No. His spirit calls him to do it. This isn't my calling. Making connections via my podcast is mine. Maybe your sweet spot is camping, organizing, blogging, podcasting, connecting, or writing. Whatever it is, you can find it and develop it over time.

The big points here are to be super intentional about honing your craft, to become an artist in whatever you do, and to nurture quality relationships. In Chapter 9, I'll give you a framework to take action in this area so you can begin to position yourself for creating more income.

Use the "Invest in Your Network" worksheet at rockretirementbook.com to create your plan.

Step 2: Position Yourself for the In-Between

Your parents' generation lived a three-stage life: education, work, retirement. This doesn't have to be how you live. Work or retirement doesn't have to be a this-or-that question. It doesn't have to be "in the rat race or out." There is an in-between where, if you prepare for it, you can thrive.

Just because you "retire" doesn't mean you're relegated to golf or hobbies. Retiring today means freeing yourself from the nine-to-five grind to pursue things you enjoy. Often, one of those pursuits is work—work you're excited about.

The in-between could be the answer to being able to retire at all or to jumping out of the rat race two to three years earlier than you'd planned. It could allow you to live life at a slower pace, a pace that gives you the time to pursue things you enjoy while earning income and keeping your options open.

Charles is a doctor. After a successful career as a surgeon, he retired in his early sixties. He was worn out from the daily grind of caring for patients and performing complex surgeries that could take ten-plus hours. When Charles retired, he still loved doctoring, so after a twelve-month retirement honeymoon, he went back to work reviewing disability claims for the US Department of Veterans Affairs. Two days a week, he reviewed charts, saw patients, and helped the VA get out from under a massive backlog of cases. It wasn't sexy, but it paid pretty well, and it allowed him the freedom to pursue other passions. Now in his mid-seventies, he recently stopped working altogether. Looking back, he's glad he stayed active in his profession. He feels that working during retirement gave him purpose. He liked having a reason to get up in the morning and using the skills he had honed over decades as a physician.

On the financial side, if you create income at any level in retirement, it can play an important part in lowering financial risks. Income during the first ten years of retirement can help preserve your assets, allow you to take less investment risk, and buy you a bigger life earlier on.

For Dr. Charles, it helped him feel more in control of his family's financial well-being. When the Great Recession hit in 2007, he stepped up his hours to help preserve his investment assets. This helped him avoid drawing assets from his accounts while the markets were depressed. He knew selling assets during a bad market could have a significant negative impact on his portfolio, and working gave him the ability to avoid that. The empowerment of earning an income also helped him manage his emotions as markets swooned. When the markets began to recover in 2009, he went back to a regular schedule without having to adjust any of the family's spending or long-term goals.

Truthfully, the most positive impact isn't the income. Working has a great psychological benefit that can make you a better investor. Working empowers you. Earning income, even if it is modest, frees you from feeling totally dependent on things you can't control, like the stock market, interest rates, and the economy. This sense of control allows you to be more patient with your investments. It gives you more flexibility in how you invest and when you tap your accounts.

Step 3: Identify Retirement Income Opportunities

The time to start planning the in-between is while you're still working full-time. Earning extra income during the first ten years of retirement may be crucial to your financial success. For reasons we've already discussed, you'll be spending more and living longer and that can be a deadly combination, financially speaking. Earning some coin could be your ticket to retiring a few years earlier, getting more of your ideal retirement, or just being able to retire. If you start planning early, you'll be *able* to do something you enjoy, earn income to preserve your nest egg, and maintain the freedom to enjoy life. What a bargain!

When your kids have moved out of the house, use the time you have while still working to experiment with ways to earn income on your own terms. There are so many ways to earn money. The key is to find one that fits with your life. Here are some ideas to get you thinking.

Take Advantage of the Sharing Economy

Even if you're not familiar with the term, you've likely participated in the sharing economy. If you've ridden in an Uber, if you've rented a vacation condo on Airbnb, if you've bought furniture on OfferUp, you've used the sharing economy. The sharing economy is a simple a way for people like you and me to find human or physical resources with those who have them. Typically it's powered by the Internet on websites that connect the buyer and the seller. What does this have to do with your having fun and earning money in retirement? Well, possibly, a lot!

No matter who you are, you have skills that people need. The rise of the sharing economy makes it easier than ever for you to connect with others who need them. Organized and computer savvy? Work as a virtual assistant, doing anything from basic admin to complex project management. A handyman? Connect with people needing home repairs via TaskRabbit. Like to drive? Be an Uber driver. Love having company? Rent a room to visitors via Airbnb. Love to cook? Cook meals for busy families. Love to teach? Tutor students locally or online. Love animals? Walk or sit animals for busy families. A design whiz? Sell your creative services online. There are so many opportunities to put your skills and passions to use and earn money. The great thing is, you're always in control. You work when you want to work. You charge what you're comfortable charging, and you only have to work with nice people.

Second-Act Entrepreneurship

Entrepreneurship may be a perfect way to simultaneously create income and personal fulfillment. Entrepreneurship among seniors is on the rise. In 2013, nearly one-quarter of all new businesses were started by people ages fifty-five to sixty-four, and Americans in this age group start new businesses at a higher rate than those in their twenties and thirties—which has been true since 1996 (Stangler 2014).

If starting a business is attractive, the data from the US Small Business Administration's Office of Advocacy shows that small businesses are started on a shoestring budget. Based on 2007 Census data, 70 percent of entrepreneurs reported using less than $25,000 in start-up capital and 44 percent started their businesses with less than $5,000 (Intuit 2017). Go big with your time and go big with your creativity, but not with your capital, because at this point in your life, you can't afford big losses.

I have a client four or five years from retirement. He has a ranch he loves to go work on each weekend. He's in a financially perilous situation, and we were talking about what he could do to earn income when he retired. He had considered starting a small landscaping company mowing lawns. His idea was to retire, take X amount of dollars, buy the equipment, and go get clients. My counsel to him was to start now and start small. How does he know he's going to want to start the landscaping company in four years? Why wait to figure it out? Test it now. Buy a used, reasonably priced lawn mower and a trailer, and go find one lawn to mow. Do it while he's working at his current job. Do one lawn on the weekend and see how that goes. He'll find out if this business is for him now rather than waiting until retirement. Then when retirement comes, if he still likes it, he's already got clientele and can expand the business. The key is a lean start-up. He can pivot time and creativity on a dime, but if he uses a lot of capital and there's a big lurch in the market, it's tough to make up the losses.

Another great aspect of testing out a business is that you can see how the business would fit into retirement. Family members in their seventies recently let me know that they were looking at a sub shop franchise and asked my advice. I pointed out that, first and foremost, you've got to pay the franchise fees. You'll also need a commercial lease and the equipment. You'll then need to hire and manage employees and likely have to work there every single day. Is that how you want to spend your retirement years? The answer was no.

Step 4: Execution

Income and purpose in retirement isn't all about dollars and cents; it's about self-worth and self-image. These concerns may not have been as important to our grandparents, but they *are* to us. We want to be "in the zone" and the best way to do that is not to watch the clock tick down until you retire, but to start thinking through where you'd like to be and putting the pieces into place.

What steps can you take to improve your cash flow situation or your income potential in the market right now? How can you intentionally network within your company to improve your future prospects? How can you design your work or business so that it provides more freedom and more income potential? Even if you ultimately choose not to create income in retirement, you'll have more options.

Go to rockretirementbook.com for the "Master the In-between" worksheet to help you plan yours.

Mastering the cash flow equation will give you a big boost in thriving outside the lines. Next we'll look at what to do with all that extra cash you've freed up.

CHAPTER SUMMARY

☐ **"Wax On"**—Your income today and tomorrow is your source of building wealth to help you create your masterpiece. You must learn to master it.

☐ **"Wax Off"**—This is all the basic expenses, the wants, and the desires that cost money. You can have all the income in the world, but if you waste it, you'll never build wealth. You must learn to master it.

☐ **The "B Word"**—According to Gallup, 68 percent of American adults don't have a budget. If you hate to budget, try Roger's Super-Simple Anti-Budget Budget.

☐ **The Income Impact**—Budgeting is important but it won't move the dial much in your financial life. To thrive, apply the income impact. Invest in your skills, work ethic, and network to become an "A" player.

☐ **Master the In-Between**—There is a space between work and retirement. It is called "freedom." Working during the first ten years of retirement can be key to creating your retirement masterpiece.

CHAPTER 7
MANAGING YOUR NET WORTH

"Make things as simple as possible,
but not simpler."

—ALBERT EINSTEIN (ATTRIBUTED)

"**Y**ou work hard for your money...so hard for it, honey...so you better treat it right!" OK, that's not quite what Donna Summers sang, but you *do* work hard for your money, and it should work hard for you too. The way you get it to work hard is by becoming a master at managing your net worth.

THE TACTIC TRAP

Many retirement books primarily focus on money tactics, things like the mechanics of insurance, 401(k)s, choosing between a Roth IRA or traditional IRA, and investment strategies. I hope I've convinced you there is much more to rocking retirement than merely money tactics. Tactics are great, but they're just tools—no different than a hammer or a screwdriver.

Focusing too much on tactics can cost you a lot of money. You try one tactic (tool), then another, and another until you end up with a collection of investments not focused on achieving anything in particular. They clutter your portfolio, making it difficult to focus on the important issues. Most importantly, a fixation on tactics distracts you from building something important—like a great life.

When you're in the growth phase of wealth creation, it's easy to look for every angle to accelerate it (and there are thousands willing to pitch you products to help). As a result, by the time many reach their fifties, their assets look like a big messy, tangled ball of yarn. Lots of different investments and tactics going in all different directions.

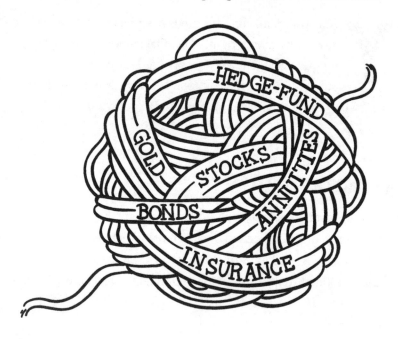

Almost all of us do this (my hand is up). When you reach your fifties, it's important that all your assets are working together. It's asset allocation from a different angle. The goal is not necessarily to make the most money in the shortest amount of time, but to take as smooth a ride as possible. How can you accomplish the most important things using money as the tool? Instead of buying the XYZ super-duper growth fund or the hot stock your brother-in-law bought or whatever else made sense at the time, you construct a shell of a portfolio, a structure, then work on what goes in it. The tool to construct that shell is your net worth statement.

THE NET WORTH STATEMENT

Your net worth statement is one of the most essential documents in managing your personal financial life. What's interesting is that most people don't keep one. The net worth statement is actually very simple. It's a one-page document that summarizes your financial life.

On the left side of the page, it lists of all of your assets:

- Bank accounts
- Investment accounts
- Retirement accounts
- Real estate
- Business interests
- Cars
- Etc.

On the right side of the page, it lists all of your debts:

- Mortgage
- Second mortgage
- Auto loans
- Consumer loans (like credit cards)
- Student loans
- Etc.

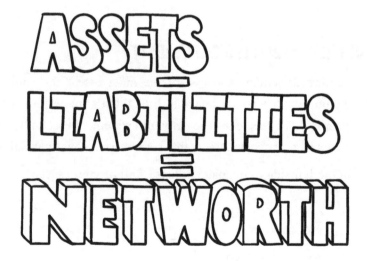

Once you list everything, add up all your assets and subtract all your debts, and that number represents your net worth. Over time, if you're saving and investing or paying down debts, your net worth number should increase. That's how you'll know you're making progress financially.

The net worth statement should focus on productive assets like those listed above, something you would sell to buy something else. I don't like to include what I call "use assets," things you need and use in your everyday life. Examples of use assets include home furnishings and cars. You may want to include a use asset on your net worth statement if there's a debt on it, but you will likely always own something like a car, so it doesn't really have a value. Creating and maintaining a net worth statement is simple.

> **If you haven't created yours yet, go to rockretirementbook.com for a "Build Your Net Worth" worksheet that will show you all the steps.**

Why I LOVE Net Worth Statements— and You Should Too

Oh, how I love the net worth statement! Let me count the ways! Seriously, I love it, and you will too by the end of this chapter (I hope). Here's why.

1. Your Personal Measuring Stick

I know this isn't nice to say, but I hate the Joneses. I do. They've always got the latest and greatest whatever. Their kids are well adjusted. Their yard has not only a sign, but a permanent plaque inscribed with "Yard of the Month . . . Forever." They always get the raise, the promotion, the medal, the trophy, and the best parking spot. What I hate most about the Joneses is what they do to my clients, to me, and possibly to you. They make us feel inadequate. In our quest to keep up with them, we make really bad decisions with money, decisions that don't allow us to rock retirement. It's time to kick the Joneses to the curb. It's time to measure our life on our own terms.

Comparing yourself to the outside world is a loser's game—and *you* are *not* a loser. Knowing your net worth is a great way to rid your life of the Joneses forever. Instead of looking outward and comparing your financial progress to that of your neighbor or the S&P 500 (things you can't control), focus inward on the progress you're making. You are on your own journey, so it just makes sense to always evaluate where you are now based on your own unique financial past.

Take John; he and I have worked together for fifteen years. When we started, he had a negative net worth statement (more debt than assets). On paper, he was broke. He was a newer professional with student loans to pay, as well as a hefty loan to set up his practice. As we began to walk life together and his income grew, I helped him make smart choices on how to allocate the extra income he earned using his net worth statement. Over time, years in fact, each of the little smart choices he made began to add up. Occasionally, John would get frustrated by his progress. Month by month, or even year by year, it can feel that way, especially when the Joneses seem to be everywhere. When John got frustrated about his financial life, I'd take him back to his net worth statement. We'd look at where he'd begun and at the graph charting his progress over the years. Over fifteen years, he'd gone from a negative net worth to being worth millions.

Look outward at the Joneses, and you'll always feel inadequate.

Look inward at your personal measuring stick, and you'll see how far you've come on your journey.

Using your net worth statement in this way grounds you. It keeps you from worrying when you don't have to and shows you where to focus if you're not where you want to be. It will identify potential problems, such as having too much cash or unproductive assets. It will also help you identify and eliminate the bad debt like credit cards, consumer loans, and auto loans.

2. Intentions vs. Actions

It's said the road to Hell is paved with good intentions. Financially speaking, the road to not rocking retirement is paved with those same good intentions. This may sound harsh, but it's true and needs to be said. We all have good intentions to save more, to build an emergency fund, to pay down that nagging credit card—and yet, most often, we don't do those things. The beauty of the net worth statement is that it cuts through all our good financial intentions and shows us the exact sum total of the actual financial decisions and actions we've taken over time. In the spirit of Ralph Waldo Emerson's famous quote, your net worth statement speaks so loudly you can't hear what you're saying. I know. I've been drowned out by my net worth statement more than I'd like to admit.

Many years ago, I worked with a super-nice guy named Justin. Justin was fifteen years my senior, very smart, and made a ton of money. For many years his annual income was north of $1 million. The dude was racking it in, yet, when we sat down and created his first net worth statement, he was worth $350,000. He was shocked.

"How could that be?" he asked. "Look at my house and car! I drive a Porsche and own a two-million-dollar home." I agreed and pointed out that the car was leased and the home had a mortgage almost equal to its value.

I said, "Justin, it's no doubt you're successful and make a lot of income, but you're not wealthy. You spend virtually every dollar you earn."

Although he was committed to changing his spending habits so he could begin to accumulate wealth, his actions never matched his good intentions.

It's like when you've made a resolution to work out more and eat healthy, but a month later, the scale tells you it hasn't happened. When you see the number on the scale, it tells you to focus more closely on your resolution to get the results you desire. In the same way, the net worth statement tells you when you're not saving as much as you'd planned, or that the emergency fund still needs investing, or that the toys you've bought over the last six months have cut into your cash flow.

Ultimately, your net worth reflects your values. You may be telling yourself or your financial advisor that you value financial security, but if you have lots of debt and buy lots of things, it's likely that your teeter-totter is tilted more toward immediate gratification. It works the other way too. You may tell yourself you want to enjoy traveling while the kids are still at home, but if all you do is save and invest, your teeter-totter is tilted more toward tomorrow. Knowing yourself is very important when you're setting financial goals, either to change what you don't like or to be honest about what you enjoy and allow for it.

3. Your Financial Dashboard

FINANCIAL DASHBOARD
YOUR NETWORTH
$2,654,620

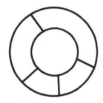

$2,805,000
TOTAL ASSETS
☐ Taxable
☐ Tax-Deferred
☐ Tax-Free

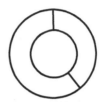

$150,380
TOTAL LIABILITIES
☐ Secured
☐ Unsecured

Like your car's dashboard, your net worth statement provides critical information about your operating status. It contains gauges like:

- Cash available

- Emergency reserves

- Value of assets by tax status

- Productive assets vs. use assets

- Debt levels

- Overall value of your net worth

As you walk through life, you can easily check your financial status by glancing at your financial dashboard. When you have a big financial decision to make, like receiving a bonus or considering a big purchase, your dashboard can help you gauge the best course of action.

I recommend going over your net worth statement every six months. Within that time, you will have captured wealth from managing your cash flow, and that biannual examination will let you figure out what to do with it. You'll be able to look at the net worth statement and answer the question, "How do I allocate the resources I have available to work toward the things I care about the most?" This small biannual conversation can help you avoid a big conversation like Justin's, where you discover you have made no progress toward what's most important to you. This small conversation allows you to fully align your financial resources to work toward your goals.

Another important time to review your net worth statement is when you are making a decision to deploy capital. Most of us collect investments and assets over time without giving consideration to how they fit in with our entire financial picture (remember those tactics?).

It's like shopping for a New Year's Eve party without planning out what you'll wear, and instead, you just stop by the store every week or so. On your first visit, you see a gorgeous purple shirt so you buy it. A week later, you find a pair of super comfortable hiking boots—*on sale* too. Two weeks later, you find a great deal on black dress pants. The next week, it's chilly out, so you buy a navy-blue peacoat. The night of the event, you put on your new outfit and discover, although each item is super cool individually, you look like . . . well, a hot mess. It's 8:30 p.m., the stores are closed, and you have no time to fix the problem. Collect investments like this, and you may reach retirement realizing you've collected a sea of misfit investments, each great on their own, but together, they're not going to cut it for the event of *your life*.

Alternatively, you could take my mom's approach. She was smart. She was a busy single mother and didn't have time to casually shop for clothes for me. She did all her shopping at Meijer's Thrifty Acres—a one-stop-shop superstore much like Walmart. She didn't have time to mix and match my clothing, so instead, she bought Garanimals. Remember Garanimals? It's a line of kids clothing with the image of an animal on the tag of each piece. When my mom bought clothes with matching animals, say a pair of pants and a shirt both with lions on the tag, she was assured that my outfit would match.

You want to build your net worth to have matching animal tags like Garanimals. When you're managing your financial assets, you want to match tags so you're assured that each investment is working toward the right goal: rocking retirement. This is your *life* we're talking about! Don't buy what's hot at the moment; build your net worth like a well-balanced wardrobe focused on the event of your life.

The rest of this chapter will give you a framework to help you build a well-designed net worth that's focused on *you.*

WALK BEFORE YOU RUN

Exercise stresses the body. It stresses your tendons, muscles, lungs, and, most of all, your mental toughness. That's why fitness trainers say you should warm up before you exercise. It helps loosen up your muscles, brings oxygen to your lungs and blood, and prepares your body for the beatdown of the workout you're about to bring on. Trainers understand that in order for you to grow from a workout, your body needs to be prepared for the stress it is about to endure.

When I first started doing endurance events like marathons and triathlons, I'd always fail miserably toward the end of each race. I'd start strong, passing lots of people, but as the race wore on, they'd begin to pass me. By the end of the race, hordes would pass me. It wasn't until I got a fancy running watch that told me how fast I was running that I realized what was happening. At the beginning of the race, when I felt fresh and strong, I'd take off at a much faster pace than I had realized, and then I'd gradually start to slow down. When I set a sustainable pace from the start, I felt like I was barely moving. It felt *slow*. But pacing yourself, especially at the beginning, is key to running a successful race. It gives you the physical and mental strength to sustain yourself as the stress of the race increases.

Managing your wealth is the same. Once you've envisioned your retirement masterpiece, it's easy to start off too strong in pursuit of it. We're so eager to get into the race and grow our wealth, we forego the warm-up and don't settle into a sustainable pace. Warming up and settling into a pace feels like we're wasting time. It feels slow, which is why few people take the simple steps I'm about to cover. Regardless of where you are in your financial journey, walking before you run is an essential step in preparing yourself to sustain a race pace when the fatigue and stress of life (and markets) sets in.

Remember, the retirement masterpiece you're creating has to last your lifetime. Here is my three step warm-up process to help prepare you for your financial race.

1. Walk First: The Emergency Fund

OK, stick with me here; I'm going to mix metaphors. Although maintaining an adequate emergency fund is the first step in warming up for your race, I like to call it your "financial airbag." There'll be lots of dangers on our journey, so it's important that you have enough liquidity to manage life's challenges; this is traditionally called an "emergency fund." Think about your car's airbag. It actually costs quite a bit of money. If you had to write a check for the $2,000 or so that it costs for an airbag, you might never have one, especially since it's a worthless asset 99.999 percent of the time you're driving . . . but when you really need it, it's literally a lifesaver.

This is why so many people don't have an emergency fund: They feel it's wasted money. It just sits there, doing nothing. There's no apparent return on investment (let's get fancy, and say "ROI"). Just like warming up before your run, it feels like a waste of time. There are so many "important" things you could do with the money. You could spend it on lifestyle. You could pay down debt. You could buy an investment. All of these decisions seem like better options than letting a lot of money just sit there doing nothing. But the ROI of an emergency fund is not in the interest rate or rate of return. Your ROI comes when life hits you like an oncoming car. That's when you really need that airbag.

And guess what? Life always happens—*always*, and if you don't have an emergency fund, your options to deal with an event are severely limited. You will either need to work harder to earn the money to cover the costs, take a hit to your current lifestyle, or borrow money to cover the unexpected costs—adding debt to your balance sheet and costs in the form of interest. You might beg, borrow, or steal from family (probably not a great idea), or sell long-term investment assets. Selling something valuable when you're desperate is the worst position to be in, because you're at the mercy of the market.

An emergency fund allows you to simply roll over those unexpected life events without scrambling and disrupting your life or being inefficient with your assets. It will give you not just security, but also the *feeling* of security, which is a gift in itself.

There are various rules of thumb recommended for the size of the emergency fund: three months, six months, or twelve months. What works for you will depend upon your comfort level, your current level of income, and your fixed expenses. The latter is important, because the higher your fixed expenses, the more important it is that those are covered; you can't dial those down when life happens.

2. Now Stretch a Little: Extraordinary Expenses Fund

Now that you're warmed up a bit, let's loosen up with a good stretch. In addition to your emergency fund, you'll want to have some cash stashed to cover bigger expenses you know are coming. Any extraordinary expenses you foresee in the next twelve months need to be accounted for.

For example, when my son and daughter entered college in the fall, I knew I'd have to pay the tuition. It's not in my normal expense cycle, so I needed to allocate funds for that over and above my emergency fund, savings, and investments. I knew I needed to sock away a little bit more to cover those expenses over the next few years without it disrupting my life. For you, it could be a vacation, new car, home remodel, or business investment. Whatever it is, if it's coming up within the next twelve months, stash the cash for it. In this way, rather than careening from event to event, shredding your nerves each time, you know what's coming and that you've taken care of it.

3. Start Jogging a Bit: Paying Bad Debt

Now for our last bit of warm-up. I know, you're raring to go, but settle down there, Skippy. You need to take care of one last thing: Pay off your bad debt. What's bad debt? Generally any debt that is on a nonexistent (think: credit card) or depreciating (think: car) asset. These debts cost you in three big ways. They charge high interest and they're easy to use, which causes you to spend more and zaps your cash flow. Loosen up that cash flow and pay them off. According to NerdWallet.com, in 2015, the average credit card balance for a US household was $15,762 (El Issa 2016). And according to CreditCards.com, the average interest rate on a credit card is 14.9 percent (Dilworth 2016). That's not just bad; that's *awful*. Before we get to race pace, let's jog a bit and get an easy win. If you have this type of bad debt, pay it off before you think about investing. Doing so will give you an immediate return on your cash by avoiding the interest charged on your debt. Free from the debt payment, you should have more money to allocate to long-term investments.

These three steps are critical to successfully managing your assets. Most people skip them. They jump right to buying investments, which is the worst thing one can do. Skip the above steps, and you'll position yourself for failure.

ALLOCATING ASSETS – INSIDE THE LINES

Once you've taken care of the basics above, you're ready to look toward long-term investments. The traditional paint-by-numbers processes may not be the best for your unique life. Let's look at a few of them and then consider how you might better approach allocating assets.

Institutionalized Advice

Most people in the financial-advice industry have a bias toward specific financial products. Most were trained as salespeople in a particular area, and when they become financial planners, they still see the world through that lens. If Joe the planner started as an insurance salesman, he would opt for an insurance product. If Sally started as an investment broker, she'd recommend traditional stocks and bonds as the solution. If Mark had experience in annuities, he'd mainly recommend annuities. If Johnny sold real estate investments, then he'd say real estate is the best choice. If Eric thinks the world is going to come crashing down, he'd recommend hedge funds, gold, or his super-safe mattress. Depending on whom you ask, you'll get advice steering you toward the product with which the advisor is most comfortable. It's not that they're bad people or have ill intent; they just see the world through a very limited lens.

As a young advisor, I listened as a very competent insurance advisor ran me through his pitch and sold me a high-cost life insurance product. I was convinced his recommended course of action made total sense. As his sales pitch faded, however, I reassessed and realized I'd purchased because I was sold . . . not because I'd been advised on the best thing to do.

I hear similar stories all the time from other people. Many "advisors" are really salespeople in disguise. The price for this type of advice is money, time, and attention that would be better spent creating your unique retirement masterpiece.

The second issue is that most financial advisors don't think like businesspeople. Although they are taught basic investing and product knowledge, few are taught the basics of advising beyond their investment offerings. Want to invest in an individual rental property? They've likely never done it and can't help you. Want to invest in a private investment? Unless it's a packaged investment vehicle they can sell, they likely can't discuss it. Considering buying a business? They've never evaluated one. Their 360 wealth management isn't really 360 degrees. They are either prohibited from discussing or are unfamiliar with financial matters outside of their firm's offerings. As a result, you end up funneled through a narrow investment channel.

Tax Deferral at All Costs

Tax deferral is a fundamental tenet of saving for retirement. The deal is, if you contribute to your 401(k) or IRA, you can avoid taxes on those contributions (they won't be counted as income). This means more money will go to work for you and possibly grow, and you don't have to pay taxes on gains, dividends, or interest. When you reach 59½, you can access these savings without penalty, but the distributions from them will be taxed as ordinary income. In theory, you'll be in a lower tax bracket. It's the foundation of the modern retirement system. This is a big reason why tax-deferred accounts hold the lion's share of most people's retirement savings. CPAs like them because they shelter income from taxes. People like them because they pay less in taxes each year. That's why as of June 2014, there were $24 trillion dollars in retirement assets (Investment Company Institute 2014).

Don't get me wrong; tax deferral is a great savings tool. The downside to it, however, is that it provides less flexibility in your financial life. First, tax-deferred assets funnel you to traditional public-investment vehicles, like stocks, bonds, mutuals, etc. These can be great assets to deploy your capital, but they're not the only assets. If these are your only savings vehicles (Roth accounts would be included in this), then your assets will naturally be in investments mostly dependent on the world markets, something over which you have virtually no influence.

Consider Marcus. He was a very successful physician. During his career, he earned a high-six-figure income and was a diligent saver. As a high-earning physician, he had two big objectives: deferring taxes and protecting assets. Inside-the-lines advice guided him to heavily invest in tax-deferred accounts in order to accomplish his goals. Once Marcus retired, however, the way he had allocated his assets became an issue. At the age of 70, nearly all of his liquid investment assets were in tax-deferred accounts. Once he turned 70½, the IRS required him to take withdrawals from his tax-deferred accounts whether he wanted to or not. His substantial tax-deferred account balance coupled with his other income sources meant that he'd have a big tax bill every year with no real flexibility to decrease it.

You don't have to be a wealthy physician to feel the burn from deferral at all costs. Normal folks use their 401(k) for retirement savings as well. The push to start saving for retirement via 401(k)s and IRAs is a noble one, but this one step forward often leads to two steps back. Studies show many participants take early withdrawals, paying tax and a 10 percent penalty, or they cash out their retirement accounts. Why? Because often they've started allocating assets to long-term investments before they complete the basic steps above.

Risky Risk Tolerance

When Clarke and I began working together, he was fifty-four and ready to create a plan to leave his career and pursue a life in which he still worked, but had more freedom. For thirty years, Clarke had worked hard, saved religiously, and invested for growth, and now he had substantial assets to rock retirement. When we reviewed the allocation of his balance sheet, it was obvious that it was the balance sheet of a sprinter. He had little cash and few bonds, and his portfolio was filled with speculative real estate and a mix of Global Growth Companies.

I mentioned this to Clarke and he said, "Oh yeah, I've never been afraid of risk. Years ago, my advisor evaluated my risk tolerance and he agreed with my assessment, so we allocated my assets in line with my risk-tolerance score. When markets go down, I just buy more and wait. They always come back. It's served me well."

I said, "Indeed it has. You've been sprinting for quite a while and have had the income to fuel your portfolio when market bumps appeared."

He replied, "Yeah, my past advisor reassessed my risk tolerance last year. He said that although I'm older, I still have a long investment time frame and my emotional ability to handle risk is still strong. He adjusted the portfolio slightly based off of my risk score."

What Clarke experienced is a best practice in financial management. The paint-by-numbers approach has a glide path you're supposed to follow based on your risk-tolerance score (age being part of it). This glide path isn't based on what you'd like in life; it's based on a computer's analysis of a generic risk-tolerance questionnaire.

Tolerating Investment Risk Just Because You Can Is NOT a Good Strategy

Fundamental to the paint-by-numbers approach is identifying your investment risk tolerance and then building a portfolio to maximize potential returns for that level of risk. This paint-by-numbers approach is fine for younger folks, but is too generic for everyone else. It cares nothing about you or the life you want to have. It only cares about what risk you can tolerate.

If you've ever invested in your 401(k) retirement plan at work or worked with a financial advisor, most likely you've taken a risk-tolerance questionnaire in order to determine your asset allocation. The questionnaire contains a series of questions designed to determine your maximum tolerance for risk, for example:

What is your objective?

A. Growth
B. Growth with Income
C. Income with Growth
D. Income

What is your risk tolerance?

A. Conservative
B. Moderately Conservative
C. Moderate
D. Moderate Growth
E. Growth
F. Aggressive

What is your time horizon?

A. 0–2 Years
B. 3–5 Years
C. 6–10 Years
D. 10+ Years

What is your investment experience?

A. Inexperienced
B. Somewhat Inexperienced
C. Somewhat Experienced
D. Experienced
E. Very Experienced

More sophisticated questionnaires will have questions designed to measure how you might react during bad markets.

These are all reasonable questions in theory, but how they're used isn't reasonable at all. Your answers are scored to determine your *maximum* tolerance for risk. This is input into a software program called an "optimizer," which builds an asset allocation designed to maximize potential returns based on your risk score. This is how that pretty asset-allocation pie chart is generated. Depending on your risk score, they'll recommend you allocate your assets to various asset classes like large stocks, small stocks, real estate, bonds, etc. Your advisor uses this recommendation to choose investment strategies to fill in the pieces of the pie.

This paint-by-numbers approach is fine for a good period of your life—when you're younger and have lot of time and income to continually invest. It also works if a big part of your retirement masterpiece is wealth transfer. But if you're a mere mortal in wealth terms, filling in the box could cause you to never achieve your retirement masterpiece.

The paint-by-numbers approach builds an optimized portfolio to attempt to maximize returns for your *maximum* risk tolerance. It's rebalanced systematically (usually annually) to assure your portfolio is always "optimized." The strategy relies on the long-term averages of the markets to play out, and you're strapped to the mast of the ship, come hell or high water. This paint-by-numbers approach will likely create a work of art that looks nothing like the retirement masterpiece you've envisioned. Here's why.

This Race Wasn't Built for Your Retirement

This institutional approach to asset management was built . . . well, for institutions. Since the mid-1970s, pension plans, foundations, and other large institutions adopted this approach and even codified it as the best practice for managing assets—a safe harbor of sorts. This was the process I learned in the Certified Investment Management Analyst program. Following this process (and documenting it) provided structure and, just as importantly, gave legal cover to boards overseeing large sums of money.

Over the last few decades, financial firms have brought this institutional approach to retail clients like you and me. Why? The approach gives big firms three important things: a great marketing pitch of using the same process the big boys use, legal cover, and a way to easily serve thousands of clients. But institutions aren't like you and me. Their masterpiece is never finished. They don't die. Their investment time frame is extremely long; ten or fifteen years is barely a season for them. They can allow as much time as necessary for the long-term averages of the markets to work for them.

You, on the other hand, have only so much time to create your masterpiece. You don't have time to wait for things to average out. The critical investment time period for you is the first ten or fifteen years of retirement. Sure, that's a long time, but nowhere near the time frame needed to hope the averages work out for you.

I've met plenty of people disenchanted with investing and financial advisors. If you set aside those who were speculating, rather than investing, and those who had incompetent advisors, the main gripe was that the process was frustrating. They said things like, "I got tired of being told that it will all work out." "He kept showing me a chart of how a dollar grew over ninety years. I kept telling him, 'I won't live that long.'" "I just can't handle another ride like 2008." "I don't care about the markets and averages; I just want to reach my retirement goals."

That last one says it all. "I just want to reach my retirement goals." You're not concerned with optimizing returns over time; you're concerned with optimizing your life, with rocking retirement. You're not an institution that never dies. You have a limited number of years on this earth, and you want to make the most of them.

The Risk-Tolerance Questionnaire Uses the Wrong Stopwatch

Using a risk-tolerance questionnaire to determine how to allocate your assets is ridiculous and won't help you rock retirement. Oh, that feels good. I've wanted to say that for years. *It's not going to help you rock retirement.* In fact, relying on one may put your retirement in jeopardy. "WHAT?!" you exclaim. Let me explain. The goal of these questionnaires is to determine your tolerance for risk (defined as volatility). So let's define "tolerance."

Tolerance (as defined by Merriam-Webster):

1. Capacity to endure pain or hardship.
2. The act of allowing something

The goal is to survive something harmful or unpleasant. This is very different from allocating your assets in order to achieve things you actually care about. The objective of this chapter is to build a framework to allocate your hard-earned assets to work for you, to be of use to you. So let me replace "tolerance" with a better word: "utility."

Utility (as defined by Merriam-Webster):

1. Fitness for some purpose or worth to some end
2. Something useful or designed for use

When you're determining how much risk to take with your investment assets, which should you focus on: your tolerance or its utility? If you use a risk-tolerance questionnaire to determine your investment portfolio, yes, it will position you to potentially optimize your returns, but it will also position you to potentially endure the maximum amount of investment loss you think you can endure.

Let me hammer this point home. The year this book was published, I turned fifty. That's an important milestone for a man. At fifty, doctors recommend a periodic colonoscopy. Yay for me! My friends tell me that colonoscopies are not a pleasant experience. No doubt, but the medical community has determined that having them starting at age fifty is the best way to identify potential issues. There is utility to it. It is useful.

Now imagine the medical community using a risk-tolerance questionnaire to decide how often I should have a colonoscopy. In that scenario, when I turned fifty, I'd go to my doctor, and she'd give me a colonoscopy-tolerance questionnaire. I'd answer seven to eight multiple-choice questions, and the nurse would enter my score into the colonoscopy optimizer and create a colonoscopy plan customized for me. If my score showed I have a high tolerance for discomfort, the colonoscopy optimizer might determine I can tolerate twelve *per year!!!* My tolerance for such an experience has *nothing* to do with the utility of having them.

Get the difference between utility and tolerance? Did I put a fine-enough point on it? Well, the standard practice of the investment industry is to determine how much risk (volatility, loss, etc.) you can tolerate and perfectly position you to likely *experience it,* whether it helps you to achieve your goals or not! Ridiculous, right? When allocating your investment assets on your net worth statement, it should be done solely to help you create the life you want.

It Ignores Cycles

August in Texas is hot. I mean *hot.* As I write this, it's 104 degrees without a cloud in the sky, and the forecast says it will be this way for the next seven days. It's too hot to run. If I'm patient though, I know that autumn is right around the corner; temperatures will come down, and I'll enjoy running again. Then, we'll enter winter. It will be a bit cold at first, but once I'm outside for a bit, it will be pure joy.

When you allocate your investment assets, you should consider the season. There are times when certain assets are hot—sometimes, too hot. When they're hot, it can feel like it will never end. It was like that with technology companies in the mid-1990s and real estate in the mid-2000s. People assumed they'd stay hot forever and piled into them. Then, there are times when assets get cold, really cold. Nobody wants them. Almost all assets were really cold in 2007 and 2008. When the winter comes for an asset class, it feels like it will never get hot again, but it does.

The paint-by-numbers institutional approach to asset management takes advantage of this by strictly rebalancing the pie chart (asset allocation). If some assets are hot, they sell some and buy the assets that are cold. This does two things: It rebalances the pieces of the pie chart to the agreed-upon sizes so your risk level is optimized, and it sells winners and buys losers. Over time, this takes advantage of the cycles of assets. This sounds very logical, and I agree, but here's the problem: This means you're invested in all the pieces always, and at their predetermined size. Whether they're cold and getting colder or hot and getting hotter, you will be in the same size . . . always. When an asset class is at a crazy-high valuation, you'll own the same amount as you would when it's at a crazy-low valuation. Why? Because the computer said it is optimal. Go back to my running example. Using the same logic, I'd have to run the exact same amount when it's 104 out as I would when it's 36. Forget that.

This strategy works over the long term—the institutional long term—but when you're in the middle of your much shorter life, sticking to this approach is emotionally difficult.

ALLOCATING ASSETS OUTSIDE THE LINES

Your life is your own unique masterpiece. There is no other like it, and it's the only one you have. When you're allocating your assets, it should be done to move you toward achieving the life you want. Clients and listeners of the *Retirement Answer Man* podcast ask questions like:

"How do I protect my assets and still grow?"

"Can we maintain our lifestyle?"

"Will we run out of money?"

"Can we afford to travel?"

"What lifestyle is possible?"

"When can I retire?"

"Will we be OK?"

"Can we gift to our kids?"

"How do we generate income?"

"How will retirement work?"

"What am I missing?"

Based on the fact that you're reading this book, I bet your questions are the same. You're more concerned about optimizing your life than your portfolio. Life maximization asks, "What's the minimum effective dose of investment risk I need to take to be in a position to achieve my goals?" The only reason to risk your hard-earned capital is if taking that risk helps you create your retirement masterpiece. Rather than trying to maximize return, why don't we maximize our comfort level or our confidence level? Let's look at the nuts and bolts of allocating your investment assets through that lens.

Some time ago I worked with a wonderful lady named Norma. Norma had just retired from a corporate position after twenty-three years. She was unmarried with two adult children who were doing fine. After retirement, she moved from the urban area she lived in to a small lakeside community well outside of a major town. In addition to her low-seven-figure 401(k) balance, she had a pension that paid her roughly $56,000 annually. Her primary goal was to maintain her standard of living. Her big question was "Will I be OK?"

In our work together, we discovered that, yes, she should be just fine. In fact, because of her assets, pension, and modest lifestyle, she had plenty of flexibility to expand her lifestyle and still maintain a portfolio allocation within her risk tolerance. We explored this more and concluded she had left no stone unturned; she was content. We also stress tested her plan against bad returns, major health events, and other such calamities. No blind spots to fill. Based on this, we agreed to take even smaller investment risk than the risk-tolerance questionnaire recommended. Actually, *a lot* smaller risk. Why? Because taking more investment risk didn't buy her anything she cared to have.

Balanced Runner

Flexibility isn't just great for athletes; it's great for your net worth statement as well. A great deal of financial flexibility comes from having tax diversification. If you're like most, the vast majority of your investment assets are in tax-deferred accounts like IRAs and

401(k)s. They're attractive while you're working because you get the benefit of not paying taxes on that portion of your income or on any of the gains, dividends, or interest you receive.

For the life-maximization race, however, it can be a poor design. Each dollar coming out of your tax-deferred account in retirement is taxed as ordinary income. If these are the only liquid investments you have, you'll likely have no choice but to draw from the pretax account and pay ordinary income taxes. If you're able to avoid drawing from these assets early on, you'll be required to do so when you turn 70½. And you'll be required to take out pretax assets and pay taxes on the distribution for the rest of your life. In theory, you'll be in a much lower tax bracket during retirement. In reality, if you're drawing from your tax-deferred accounts, you probably won't be. I've encountered many clients whose only liquid assets are their retirement accounts. Once they reach retirement, they want to know how to fund their lifestyle. With only tax-deferred assets, they have little choice but to take a distribution from their retirement account and pay the taxes no matter what it is going to cost them.

To manage taxes during retirement, you need to be a balanced runner. This means making sure your balance sheet has a healthy mix of after-tax, tax-free and tax-deferred investments. This will give you greater flexibility to maximize your life by mixing the categories you draw from during retirement.

Run with the Wind at Your Back

There's a usual route I run near my house. It runs north–south along the freeway. I always start out heading south along the service road. Depending on how far I'm running, I'll turn around and head north at one of three overpasses. Where I live, the wind typically comes from the south so the first half of my run is into the wind.

Investing for wealth maximization is sort of like that. We focus on the price of our assets and gauge how fast they're running. We invest for "growth," which means we're likely to feel the joys and pains of the market's ups and downs. It feels like we fight for each inch of progress we make, only to have a big gust of a market pullback take it all away. Over time, we make progress, but it's not easy.

As hard as my run south is, when I make the turn north, each stride becomes easier as the wind pushes me along. When you make the turn from wealth to life maximization, it helps if you, too, have the wind at your back. That wind is income.

Income from investments has historically been a major contributor to total returns. Bonds are an easy example of where income (in the form of interest) represented nine-tenths of the returns received. What comes as a surprise to many is the role income (from dividends) plays in the total return for equities. For example, if you purchased one share of the S&P 500 stock index (about $85) in January 1970, it would have grown to $8,133 by December 2014. Without the dividends, however, it would have grown only to $2,059 (Thornberg 2015).

Secondly, income provides an important cushion during bad markets. Even as prices of assets fluctuate up and down, income from interest, dividends, and other sources remain pretty constant. This provides cash flow even during bad markets. Even when the economy has struggles, companies that pay dividends are very reluctant to cut dividends.

Thirdly, historically, income from real estate and equity dividends rises over time. Over a fifty-one-year period (1960–2011), the S&P 500 has had an average annual increase in its dividend of 5.4 percent annually (Van Knapp 2012). This provides a hedge against inflation that the fixed-interest payments from bonds don't provide. In retirement, leaning toward assets that historically have provided a steady and growing income stream will help you achieve your goals.

Find a Comfortable Pace

The average age of an Olympic athlete is around 23½ years old. Why is that? Why don't you see forty- or fifty-year-old sprinters? You'd think more mature bodies and experienced athletes would have an advantage, but they don't. The fact is, younger athletes can handle the stress sprinting puts on their bodies. They have high energy levels, are more limber, and can quickly bounce back from injury. As an athlete grows older, these abilities diminish.

It's much the same with us. When we're younger, we've got lots of energy to work, our income is growing, and we can work our way out of most financial injuries. As we approach retirement, each of these advantages diminishes.

When you're approaching retirement, two very important things change financially. First, you're entering a time when your earnings will likely decrease or disappear. That's a big deal. Bigger than most people realize. Remember the time you bought your first car with your own money? It felt empowering. Earning income helps you feel in control. It gives you a sense of accomplishment. When you see something you desire, you work in order to buy it. When you have a financial setback, you work to make up for it. Your ability to do that goes away when you retire. The ability to earn your way toward something (or out of something) fades away. This impacts how you approach money. When you're suddenly dependent on the assets you've saved, it's disempowering. You become dependent on interest rates, the economy, and countless other forces over which you have no control.

Second, rather than slowly adding to your investment assets, you begin to draw from them. This is another big deal. Much has been written about the power of dollar-cost averaging (DCA), the system to build wealth. It involves investing a set amount consistently over a very long period of time. When markets go down, that same amount buys more shares at lower prices. When markets go up, that same amount buys fewer shares. Over time, this strategy can help accelerate your wealth building. Owning a portfolio that is volatile (goes up and down a lot) works well with this kind of strategy. It gives you the chance to buy lots of shares every time the markets go down. When you're nearing or in retirement, this superpower turns against you. Volatility becomes your kryptonite. When you draw from your assets and markets go down, you'll have to sell more shares to get the same amount out. This means when markets recover, you'll have fewer shares to increase in price. Studies have shown that volatility is not your friend in retirement. In fact, if you have bad markets near the beginning of retirement, it could put your entire retirement in jeopardy.

In this compressed investment time frame, long-term averages don't always average out. You could experience an unseasonably warm or cold period that could drastically impact your life. How different could the seasons be? Consider all the ten-year periods between 1950 and 2015 (there were 672 of them) for a 70 percent stock, 30 percent bond asset allocation. Although the average annual ten-year return was 9.3 percent, the best ten years gave you an average annual return of 16.9 percent, and the worst ten-year average annual return was –0.7 percent per year. The lucky lady who retired at age sixty at the beginning of the best ten-year period would have had an average annual return of 16.9 percent. By age seventy, if she was living a reasonable lifestyle, she likely had more money than when she started. In contrast, if the lady isn't so lucky, she could retire at the beginning of the worst ten-year period, when the same allocation lost, on average, almost 1 percent per year (0.7 percent). In this case, she'd face really tough choices.

In retirement, avoid the risky risk-tolerance approach and work to find the minimum effective dose of risk to help you achieve the life you want.

CHOOSING INVESTMENTS

You'd think this would be the easiest part of the book for me to write. I manage client assets and help them with exactly this topic all day, every day. In reality, this is the hardest part of the book from my standpoint. This isn't an investment book. It's a book about taking back control of your financial future and learning to thrive in an ever-changing world. So rather than dive deep into the seas of investment theory, let's focus on some wisdom I've acquired over twenty-five years of study, trial, error, more study, more trial, etc. What follows isn't prescriptive; I'm not going to tell you what you should buy. If you want that, there are plenty of sales brochures masquerading as books. What I will do is give you my insights on how to "think" about allocating your hard-earned capital to work toward thriving outside the lines, and then offer you a framework for how to do so.

Invest in Yourself

Your intangible assets may not show up on your net worth statement, but they can be one of the best places to deploy your capital. Your intangible assets are things like your skills, relationships, and health. Often they offer the best potential return on investment, yet I rarely see people focus here.

In Chapter 6, I talked about the big impact investing in your skills and network could have on your income and some ways to identify opportunities. It's during the net worth discussion that you decide how much capital to invest in what opportunity. It could be taking a certification course or hiring a professional coach to improve your presentation or speaking skills. A course on Excel spreadsheets, HTML, or other advanced skill online or at a local university could have an enormous return on investment.

> ## Go to rockretirementbook.com
> ## for a resource on hard and soft skills
> ## in which you can invest.

John was stuck in his law practice. Although he was a great trial attorney, it was stressful work and the hourly billing was brutal. He loved the law, but couldn't continue at the same pace and keep his family too, so he decided to change. He had always been a foodie. He loved the excitement of discovering new restaurants and would chat with the owner and chefs about their new concepts. One day he just decided, *I'm going to be the top food and beverage attorney in*

Texas. He then went about investing in the skills and network that type of attorney would need. He started talking to restaurant owners about the legal issues they faced. He researched case law in the area and began publishing articles in restaurant trade journals. He joined the local food and beverage association. As his knowledge and reputation grew, he began speaking at food and beverage conferences. Fast-forward to five years later. He is now known, not just in Texas, but also nationally, as the food and beverage law expert. His clients include winners of *Top Chef* and fast-growing concept restaurants.

Michael, on the other hand, wanted to leave his career. Although he had been in manufacturing for twenty years, he wanted to do something else. He wanted something that would allow him to help people and have more free time. While still in his day job, he decided to invest in a Christian coaching program through Professional Christian Coaching Institute. He also joined a "mastermind group" that had many successful coaches as members. Although the group cost money, he saw the value of walking life with people who were already successful in coaching. Once he earned his certification, his connections helped guide him in setting up his practice and acquiring clients. Two years later, Michael was able to leave his manufacturing job and now is a full-time Christian counselor. Although he doesn't earn as much as before, he loves his work, has more free time, and has extended his working life by doing something he loves.

Then there was Beth. She was three years from retirement. She and her husband lived in a medium-sized town in central Georgia. During one of our little conversations to review their net worth, we discussed how to deploy their excess cash reserves. They had already accumulated a portfolio of mutual funds in their taxable and tax-deferred accounts. Over the years she had expressed interest in buying income properties in their town, but had never had the time to commit to it. Her dad had owned rental property during his retirement, and she thought it would be a good thing to consider. After some discussion, we agreed to deploy a portion of their excess cash to an account dedicated to the purchase of one rental property. We set an action plan in place for her to conduct market research, find a property manager, and drive neighborhoods. Fast-forward to three year later. Beth retired and had two paid-for rental homes with plans to buy two more. This strategy allowed her to diversify away from public-market investments and generate income to fund her retirement, and gave her more control over their financial future.

These are just a few examples of how investing in yourself can have huge returns. Like any investment, there needs to a clear business case for spending the money and measuring the return you aim to receive for your investment.

Use Investments, Not Investment Products

I've probably sat through thousands of presentations by investment firms, outlining various investment strategies. By the end of the meetings, it was hard to argue with the logical case they presented about their strategy. While they all sounded great, almost all of them weren't; great presentations do not make great investments.

Some years ago, on behalf of a client, my business partner Phil and I drove to Waco, Texas, to spend a day with an investment firm offering a strategy that claimed to deliver returns in excess of 10 to 15 percent per year, had no exposure to equity markets, and maintained a "long history" of solid performance. Sounds great, right? On our drive home after seven hours of meetings with the firm's CEO and key investment people, Phil and I were stumped. It all made sense. We looked at the strategy from several angles and couldn't poke a hole in it; still, something didn't seem right.

After about ten minutes of silence I said, "Something feels wrong about it and just because we can't identify the risk, doesn't mean it's not there."

Phil agreed and we passed on the offer.

Postscript: The firm closed a few years later after a lengthy investigation by federal regulators.

That is an extreme example. More likely, a great-sounding strategy underperforms due to high fees and/or poor execution. That's why my philosophy is to use simple investment vehicles as much as possible. The further away you get from the actual investment, the higher the fees and more hidden gotchas. This sounds simple, but it's harder than you think. Like the food industry, which has taken food and turned it into food product, the financial industry has done the same. For example, vanilla wafers.

Even though they have that yummy vanilla taste, there's actually no vanilla in them! Check it out:

Ingredients: Unbleached enriched flour (wheat flour, niacin, reduced iron, thiamine mononitrate (vitamin B1), riboflavin, folic acid, sugar, canola oil, high-fructose corn syrup, partially hydrogenated cottonseed oil, whey (from milk), eggs, natural almond flavor, natural and artificial flavor, salt, leavening (baking soda, and/or calcium, phosphate), emulsifiers (mono- and diglycerides, soy lecithin)

The finance industry does the same thing. Fund companies have turned to derivatives to gain exposure to actual securities. Derivatives are the artificial flavoring of the financial world. Things like equity futures contracts, credit default swaps, interest rate swaps, reverse repurchase agreements, futures contracts, forward contracts, etc., are like the vanilla wafer. A fund can have the flavor of owning large stocks without having to have many, if any, of them in their portfolio. They'll likely say these tools allow them to gain exposure to an asset for a lot less cost and much more flexibility. I'm betting that's the same logic for no vanilla in that yummy wafer.

In addition to traditional investments moving away from organic investments, there are massive financial factories. Factories creating the financial equivalent of Twinkies. Things likes equity indexed annuities, variable annuities, leveraged and inverse ETFs, market neutral strategies, hedge fund strategies, and many more. These investment Twinkies are typically created to meet the emotional need of the day. Fearful of the equity markets? The equity-indexed-annuity salesman shouts, "Step right up!" Worried about inflation? "We've got some 2x energy ETFs that will do the trick!"

Don't get me wrong; they're not all bad. In fact, occasionally I use manufactured investments in my practice. Like eating manufactured food though, they shouldn't make up the majority of your investment diet.

Find a Free Agent

I mentioned above that most advisors are institutionalized, but not all. There is a small but growing segment of financial planners who are very competent businesspeople and financial managers. Here's how to find and engage them.

First, hire a fiduciary whose compensation only comes from you. Whether it's a flat-fee, annual retainer, or a fee based on assets under management, his or her compensation should come solely from you. This will help eliminate many conflicts of interest in the advice he or she provides. When there is a potential conflict of interest, it should be clearly disclosed.

Working with a fiduciary isn't enough. Fiduciary doesn't necessarily equal competency. Even an advisor working as a fiduciary can still have an institutionalized mind-set. I suggest finding an advisor who has a businessperson's mind-set, someone who can read financial statements and understand cash-flow and balance-sheet management. This type of advisor will be equipped to help you thrive outside the lines of institutionalized advice.

These advisors are out there. I count myself as one. To find yours, you'll need to be thorough in interviewing advisor candidates.

Go to rockretirementbook.com for an
interview template with questions to ask.

THE SCIENCE AND ART OF RAFTING: AN INVESTING FRAMEWORK

Investing is like the art of navigating a river. Think of the river as the world economy, which, like a river, has a natural current. The current for the world economy is growth. Sometimes the current is strong, and the economy grows fast. Sometimes it's slow, and every so often rapids appear which disrupt growth and stall the natural current—a recession or bear market. The world economy is wide and made up of lots of different assets: stocks, bonds, real estate, currencies, commodities, etc. Each has its own average current (rate of return) and rapids profile (risk). Bonds are typically near the bottom and edges of the river, where the current is slow and the water is calm. Stocks, on the other hand, are near the surface, the most volatile part of the river, where the current is fast and the rapids can be fierce.

Find Your Spot in the River

Your first decision is where in the river you need to be to create your retirement masterpiece. There is a great deal of data and academic research about the markets and world economy. The science on how to build a portfolio is robust and focuses on choosing the proper asset allocation or mix of investment assets based on the ride you'd like to take.

If you want a fast ride, you'd race right smack down the middle of the river. In investing terms, this would be 100 percent in stocks. Using the S&P 500 as a proxy, on an average year from 1951 to 2015, you'd average a return (or current) of 12.5 percent. During the fastest year for the river (or stock market), you would've raced ahead with a return of 61.2 percent. WOW, what a ride! But when you hit the worst rapids, you would have capsized your boat and lost 43.3 percent. Get the picture?

The opposite extreme is drifting along the banks of the river. This would be akin to investing only in bonds. Though the ride is usually boring, you hardly ever get wet. Of course, you'd hardly make any progress either. The average annual current here from 1951 to 2015 (measured by the Intermediate Treasury Bond Index) was 5.9 percent. Its fastest year would have moved you along with a return of 28.6 percent, with its slowest year being –3.9 percent (Atalanta Sosnoff 2016).

There are lots of asset classes that make up the river of the world economy. These include (but aren't limited to):

- US Large-Growth Stocks
- US Large-Value Stocks
- US Small-Growth Stocks
- US Small-Value Stocks
- International Developed Stocks
- Developing Market Stocks

- US Government Bonds (short-, medium-, long-term)

- US Corporate Bonds (various maturities and credit ratings)

- International Bonds

- US Real Estate (residential, retail, office, industrial, etc.)

- International Real Estate

- Commodities

- Precious Metals

- Currencies

Each has a unique current (average return), ripples (risk or standard deviation), and interacts with the others differently (correlation). Developing your asset allocation strategy is about choosing the right place on the river or the right mix of assets to help you create your retirement masterpiece while being able to stay in the boat when the rapids hit.

Based on your personal race goals, you'll need to choose an asset allocation with an average current strong enough to move you toward your finish line, but one that keeps you dry enough to enjoy the ride.

Riding the River

You can ride the river with passive investing. Passive investments use a low-cost ETF or mutual fund that mimics an index like the S&P 500. They're typically super-low cost, as well as tax efficient, and have no guide other than the index they represent. Using only passive strategies is like riding the river on Huck Finn's raft; it's a basic craft, a bunch of logs strapped together with twine. You push yourself into the spot in the river you're comfortable with and float along with the current. Every now and then, as you float a bit off your chosen course, you nudge yourself back. When the current is stagnant, you'll be stagnant. When the rapids come, you hit them, feeling the full force based on where you are in the river.

Over time you should get close to market returns and market risk consistent with your target allocation (less expenses and taxes). The advantages of this strategy are that your expenses should be low (a big advantage), you'll maintain a consistent risk/return profile, and you'll always know exactly what you own.

Navigating the River

There are two basic types of active management. First there's the more popular traditional active approach. Rather than ride on a basic raft straight down your course on the river, the active approach attempts to ride the same course, but with a more streamlined vessel. Instead of on a Huck Finn raft, you ride in a boat. The boat is managed by a maintenance person. His job is to maintain the boat and try to make it ride well on the course of the river you've chosen. Now, unlike a raft, a boat costs money, and the maintenance person has to be paid. Your bet is that spending the extra cash gets you a well-maintained boat that moves down the river faster.

In investment terms, this is traditional active management. Rather than buy funds that mimic unmanaged indexes, you select funds with managers who try to select the most attractive securities for each piece of your allocation.

Traditional active management plays a game of inches. They tie themselves to a spot in the market, stay fully invested there, and try to add value by stock selection. For example, an actively managed large-cap fund will invest in large company stocks and be compared to the S&P 500 index. They'll stay fully invested in that spot, regardless of value. In fact, most tie themselves so closely to their index counterpart, they have very little room to maneuver. If the S&P 500 has 20 percent in financial stocks, the traditional active manager will have roughly 20 percent in financial stocks, regardless of whether they're a good investment or not. A big bet against, say, financial stocks, might be to underweight them by having 17 percent in them rather than 20 percent.

This and other such limitations make traditional active management a bad deal. Numerous studies have shown traditional active managers can't overcome the added expenses needed to cover their fees. Most asset-management companies support a massive corporate structure focused as much (or more!) on marketing their portfolios as managing them.

The second approach to active asset management is one I feel has utility; remember that word? It's called Strategic Active Management. Unlike the traditional game of inches, Strategic Active Managers are given freedom. They work to add value not just in security selection, but also in leaning toward perceived undervalued assets and away from perceived overvalued assets, and have the ability to lean toward cash if they can't find attractive assets. I use these as a complement to a core portfolio of more passive investments. This portion serves two purposes: to work to increase the income generated and to lower volatility.

I won't prescribe any here. The ones you choose should be based on you and your unique retirement masterpiece.

A Word of Caution

Don't fall into the tactic trap and get too fancy in what you do with your wealth. The tactic trap will lead you on an endless chase trying to catch the "right" investment. It's a fool's errand that won't help you reach your goals.

You work hard for your money. It takes a lot of work and a lot of years to build wealth. When you're deciding how to make it work for you, make sure you use a sound framework to help guide you. Your net worth statement is that. It's a great way to monitor liquidity, tax buckets, investments, and debt levels. Over time, it serves as your personal benchmark, showing you the end result of all your little money decisions.

Phew, this is a heavy chapter. Let's move back to designing, dreaming, and implementing your retirement masterpiece.

> ## Go to rockretirementbook.com and complete the "Build Your Net Worth" worksheet.

CHAPTER SUMMARY

☐ **Net Worth Statement**—Your net worth statement serves as your financial dashboard. In one place, you can monitor the allocation of your resources and track your progress. Growing your net worth is a better personal measuring stick than the markets. It is a direct reflection of all your saving and spending decisions.

☐ **Walk Before You Run**—Take these basic steps before investing:

☐ **Walk First**—Build an emergency fund to give you liquidity to handle life's unexpected events.

☐ **Stretch**—Forecast extraordinary expenses and allocate cash twelve months in advance to pay for them.

☐ **Jog**—Pay off all your bad debt to eliminate interest expenses and reduce monthly payment obligations.

☐ **Investing Inside the Lines**—Traditional investment advice limits your options. Most financial advisors practice groupthink around investment products and are not business savvy. Tax deferral at all costs can limit your financial flexibility in retirement. And the best practice of establishing your risk tolerance and allocating your assets can actually set you up for failure.

☐ **Investing Outside the Lines**—Build investment assets in all the tax buckets to give you more flexibility during retirement. Income from investments gives you an element of consistency in your investments, an essential element as you grow older. Target a minimum effective dose of investment risk to help you achieve your goals.

☐ **Investing**—Investing in yourself can be one of the best investments you can make. As much as possible, choose investments over investment products. If you want to work with an advisor, use an undefended advisor that acts as a fiduciary.

CHAPTER 8

THE NEGOTIATION —GETTING TO POSSIBLE

"Desires dictate our priorities, priorities shape
our choices, and choices determine our actions."

—DALLIN H. OAKS, LAW PROFESSOR
AND UTAH SUPREME COURT JUSTICE

R emember back in Chapter 5 when I challenged you to think big about your life? I encouraged you to stop being so reasonable and to dream up your retirement masterpiece. That's step one for a reason. I want you to dream about your future life without the chains of your current life circumstance. I didn't want you to kill your dreams before you've dreamed them. Hopefully you took the challenge and created a vision of a life so big it might scare you a little—maybe even a lot! If so, congrats, you did awesomely!

If you had trouble thinking big about your future, you're not alone. Maybe you said to yourself, *This Roger guy is crazy.*

Dreaming big is fine, but I want to create a realistic vision, not some pipe dream. You're right. Life is a series of trade-offs. Your dream may not be possible, or better said, you may not want to walk the journey to work toward it, not because you can't or aren't brave enough, but because you've cast the vision, inventoried your resources, determined the cost (financially and personally), and decided you value other things in life more.

But I caution you not to make that determination before you've cast your dream. If you felt like you were holding back, go back and reread Chapter 5. Take another shot. This is the only life you've got; don't waste it. Once you've done that, come back here, and then be reasonable.

This step is the process of negotiation—taking that ideal vision of your life, prioritizing it and negotiating to achieve what's most important. Negotiating retirement will help you squeeze as much enjoyment and movement out of your active years as possible.

"Wait a second," you say, "Prioritize? Negotiate? You had me dream big. I can picture my masterpiece in my mind. It's awesome. Why can't I have it all??" Yeah, I know. It would be great to have it all. If you can have it all, you're either super wealthy or didn't dream big enough. For most of us though, we're dealing with limited resources. We can't have it all. Or possibly don't want to do what it takes. By dreaming "it all" first though, you can prioritize your life's desires to focus on the ones you care about most. By getting those desires down, hopefully you've expanded your vision of what your future could be, thus expanding the options before you. Negotiating isn't giving up; it's prioritizing in order to choose what's most important to you so you can take action and create a retirement masterpiece as epic as possible.

NEGOTIATION - INSIDE THE LINES

If you stay inside the lines of the paint-by-numbers approach, you will probably not like the negotiation. It sees your art (life) as a basic math problem. If their math says you can't reach your goals, the solutions are limited. It's a simple multiple-choice answer key:

A. Save more (sacrifice more of your life right now).

B. Take more investment risk to reach for returns.

C. Get better investments.

D. Work full-time for longer.

E. Lower your spending goals for all of retirement.

F. A bit of all of the above.

These are the lines of the paint-by-numbers image someone else created for you—not too creative and all really poor, uninspired choices. Yet, every day, this is the basic choice set used. People plan their lives within these lines. As a result, many say no to more life now, endure market gyrations they never wanted, fall for investment products, stay at work longer, settle for getting by in retirement, or suffer a bit of all of these things. Every day, people like you are funneled down a path where they have little control and limited options. Not an ideal path for masterpiece creation.

NEGOTIATION - OUTSIDE THE LINES

Now let's explore outside the lines. Outside the lines, your choices explode, limited only by your imagination and courage.

This can be a bit intimidating. The paint-by-numbers approach seems safe. It provides a false sense of security on what retirement will look like even if it's not one you enjoy. Recall that in Chapter 4 I pointed out that staying inside the lines doesn't take away the uncertainty. Be brave. You can do this.

Every artist is constrained by time and resources. When you create your retirement masterpiece, you will be too. Achieving the possible requires thinking creatively about how much of your ideal you can squeeze out of your time and resources. It's a negotiation where you prioritize and create. Your negotiation takes into account retirement age, working in retirement, lifestyle budget, wants and wishes, current savings rate, estate planning, investment risk, and turning use assets into productive assets. All the elements work together, and you can trade to achieve the perfect balance, your ideal retirement.

As with most things, there's no free lunch. If retiring early is an essential, you'll have to be willing to negotiate away something else to offset it. When I work with clients, I call these the "messy meetings." In these meetings I help clients prioritize, negotiate and test out multiple scenarios. With couples you have the added dynamic of two people, which adds a whole new layer. At its best, it's fun to see each spouse openly discussing their vision for their life together and forming a joint vision in a safe place. At its worst, it can bring to the surface long-lingering misalignments; these are bigger conversations.

Retirement Age

For some, the age they leave full-time work is nonnegotiable; for others, it isn't. When you choose the date, also define how important that date is to you. Is it a ten (must have) or a five? Your ideal retirement age may be fifty-five, but you'd be happy with age sixty as well. The additional five years change how the numbers work dramatically. Not only do you get five more years of earnings and savings with the later retirement date, but also these are typically your highest-earning years. If retirement at fifty-five is a must have (a deal-breaker), then it's likely something else has to give. It could be adjustments in your lifestyle, current savings rate, estate planning, investment risk, or working in retirement. A lower retirement age might necessitate a concession in one or more of those areas.

Working in Retirement

As we've discussed before, we've been conditioned to think of work and income as an either/or proposition. It's not. Working doesn't have to be like a light switch: on or off. More people are finding that they can dim their work life to a level they enjoy and gain the freedom to pursue life outside of work. I often hear it's not work they want to leave; it's work's harsh glare that washes out the rest of their lives. Today you have more options than ever before to dim work just enough to create a balanced scene for you to thrive in. If this fits you, it could buy you the ability to retire from full-time work years earlier, take less investment risk, save less now, or support higher spending. Just like retirement age, there are big dollars at play here. Each dollar you bring in working in retirement helps you live a richer life in other areas. See how venturing outside the lines can help you create your retirement masterpiece?

Lifestyle Budget During Retirement

Each of us has a unique basic lifestyle budget. I've seen couples who have everything they want spending $50,000 per year. I've also seen

180 | ROCK RETIREMENT

individuals spend $200,000 annually on the basic necessities. How high your number is will determine how much you may need to give in other areas. Looking at your ideal retirement lifestyle budget from Chapter 5, how important is it? Did you think so big that even though you dreamed of $240,000, in reality you'd be tickled pink living on $120,000 annually? Frame your lifestyle budget with one that allows you to live at an acceptable level. For example, if $240,000 ($20,000 monthly) is your dream, but you'd be perfectly comfortable with $120,000 ($10,000 monthly) then use that. Don't get caught up in the number of zeros; we're each unique.

I want to spend a bit more time here to point out one of the biggest flaws I see in retirement planning. The inside-the-lines approach assumes you'll spend at the same level from the time you retire until you die. In my experience, people don't spend like that, and this assumption can take a significant toll on your negotiation. For example, assume you're age sixty, and you want that ideal budget of $240,000 annually during retirement. An inside-the-lines approach would increase it each year by inflation (say, 3 percent) until you die (say, age ninety). Each year the plan would increase your spending by 3 percent. Though this seems reasonable, it typically isn't. Over time, the assumed cost of your initial $240,000 annual budget skyrockets. Just look:

- At age 60 it would be $240,000
- At age 65 it would be $278,226
- At age 70 it would be $322,540
- At age 80 it would be $433,467
- At age 90 it would be $582,543!!!

This simplistic spending assumption could drastically overestimate your lifestyle budget, causing you to negotiate away things you care about in order to make the numbers work. You'd need a huge nest egg to start to hit those numbers.

In reality, almost no one spends that way. Life is more nuanced than that. Research shows that although spending starts off strong in the early stages of retirement, it slows down as we age. It makes sense when you think about it. In the early stages, you are healthy, more active, and experiencing life. As you age, you naturally settle into a more relaxed pace.

Retirement can be divided into three cycles or phases. The Go-Go years are those years in which you are the most independent, free, healthy, and active, usually early in retirement. You're the most energetic and pushing yourself the hardest in this cycle. You are experiencing things and doing activities you've been putting off "until I retire" like traveling, playing golf, pursuing hobbies, or doing whatever it is that floats your boat. While you're active and out in the world, you'll likely be spending money—more money than in any other phase of retirement.

At some point, and it's a different time from person to person, but often in your mid-seventies, you will transition into the Slow-

Go cycle of retirement. You may not be as healthy as you were in your Go-Go years, or perhaps you've gone everywhere you want to go, and you settle in a bit more, enjoy your family and your partner, and relax in the home you've made. It's a bit like the transition from college to young adulthood. College was parties every night, but after a while, it got, well, old. In your Slow-Go years, you'll likely spend less on travel, hobbies, and entertaining. The amount of the spending difference will depend on your individual situation, but knowing there will be slowdown makes a big difference in the planning.

In the No-Go years, usually starting in your 80s, barring major medical issues and long-term–care events, you'll be doing a lot less and spending a lot less. Rather than dashing around the world, you might prefer a rousing game of canasta midafternoon, a nap before dinner, and a quiet evening swapping stories. Spending in the No-Go years significantly slows.

Go-Go, Slow-Go, and No-Go are natural and common transitions in how people live and spend, and it makes sense to use them to model your retirement planning. The biggest benefit is buying yourself more "go-go" in the Go-Go years. It may sound like a small distinction, but in terms of how the numbers work, it can have a huge effect on how you live out your life. It can allow you to really pursue what you enjoy in the Go-Go years, knowing you'll need less in the Slow-Go and No-Go years. It also builds in another benefit you can enjoy right now. Planning on a linear spending scale requires a big war chest to dole out in equal increments over time. If you acknowledge the spending cycles of retirement, you may not need to save as much now for that war chest. Saving less now means you can spend more today, even as you plan for retirement.

There are risks to planning in cycles, of course, because life happens. You may overspend in the Go-Go years, or perhaps you're lucky enough that your Go-Go years last longer than you had thought they might. Perhaps you'll end up with such a new and exciting career you can't resist working in the Go-Go years, or perhaps the numbers didn't hit the projections. Like a flight plan, your retirement plan can't be set in stone. You can't just point your plane in one direction and assume you'll get to the right destination safely. You need to make adjustments for wind speeds, weather patterns, and other air traffic as the flight progresses. Those same adjustments are necessary in your retirement planning no matter how you approach it. Retirement is never a "set it and forget it" proposition.

Wants and Wishes

All those wants and wishes you identified while dreaming up your ideal retirement are items for negotiation. Often we don't break our goals down that way, which makes it harder to find a good solution later on down the line. Only when you realize you can't have it all can you truly prioritize what matters most. To reach an achievable deal, you can consider scaling back and/or eliminating some items on your list. Perhaps that annual travel budget is just fine at $10,000 rather than $15,000, if it buys you retiring a year earlier. Or maybe you don't need that sailboat if you can take less investment risk as a result. Or perhaps leaving money to your kids at the end of your life is easy to let go of, if it means you can move closer to them now. There are countless adjustment options to reach a deal right for you.

Current Savings Rate

Your current savings rate is what you're saving for retirement right now. The inside-the-lines approach seems to be that regardless of how much you're saving, you should save more. As a result, you feel guilty you're not doing "enough." I say hogwash!!! Each dollar of savings now is a dollar you can't spend on living your life today. The amount you save should match your priorities. Saving for saving's sake doesn't serve anyone. If you're reading this book, I'm guessing you're likely already a saver (who else would read this book?). The non-savers are too busy watching TV or going out to eat every day. If I'm right, you don't have a savings problem, but you might have a too-much-savings problem. I've known couples who've denied themselves simple pleasures like family vacations and other occasional pleasures in order to save for retirement, not realizing they were already right on track. The saving habit is a curious thing. Those who have it always think more is better. Much of this comes from not having the perspective to know how much they need. As the savings amount adjusts up and down, it changes how you live today. You can save every last discretionary cent and miss the present, and that would be a shame. The key is to make an intentional decision on the amount you sacrifice today in order to save based on working toward the things you actually value.

Each year, I have a meeting focused on this issue with one couple I work with. The husband is so hardwired to save, he needs confirmation that it's OK to spend a certain amount on living a bit better today. His wife loves the meetings, and over time, it's been a joy to see him relax and come to love them too.

Estate Planning

How much do you want to leave at the end of your life for your family or charity? For some people, it's zero. Winning for them is making it to the finish line with nothing left in the tank. Some people want to leave money for their kids. For others, it's an institution or cause they're passionate about. It's a personal decision. Leaving an estate will have a big impact on your negotiation. That's why most people I encounter have it as "it would be nice" on their list of priorities. It is often the first thing to get traded away.

Investment Risk

Investment risk here is defined as how much your portfolio goes up and down with various markets. It's also called "volatility." As I explained in the last chapter, it's important to switch focus from wealth maximization to life maximization. My view is that you should endure enough investment risk to position you to achieve what you care about. If, however, an important goal is not risking potential losses by investing, that's OK. For some of my clients, this was one of their most important goals. They just weren't willing to handle the volatility of even a conservatively allocated portfolio. If this is you, that's cool. It's important to understand the trade-off of this priority. It could mean you may be working a bit longer, living on less, or saving more, or even all three. I've worked with clients who've made that trade-off and are perfectly happy.

Turning Use Assets into Productive Assets

A use asset is just that, an asset you use for enjoyment. Your home, condo, boat, cars, etc., are all examples of use assets. They give you joy, but contribute little, if any, economic benefit. A productive asset is one that can be used to help fund your retirement; investments that can grow in value and/or generate income.

After years of building a life and family, it's easy to approach retirement with a boatload of use assets. The most common one is a large home, one big enough to support a growing family. It likely has a game room, outdoor pool, and plenty of room for kids to play outside and in. Other common use assets I see are lake houses, cabins, condos, and other retreats.

These are all items to be considered as you plan your retirement. Whether it's not selling them at all, enjoying them for a period in retirement before converting to productive assets, or converting them now, they are important to consider as you plan your future.

GETTING TO POSSIBLE

Notice that I call it "getting to possible" rather than "finding the answer." Finding the answer is like gaining certainty: It's impossible to achieve. "Getting to possible" is the best you're going to get. As we discussed in an earlier chapter, uncertainty is the only certainty. Embrace this and focus on negotiating a "possible" that's focused on the things you care about most.

One big mistake I see people and planners make is planning too much. They'll spend hours, even days fine-tuning each assumption and building spreadsheets to forecast in detail each year's actions. This may work when designing a widget or building, but your life is not an engineering project. Your life is fluid, constantly changing directions based on the currents of the world and your desires.

Detailed planning gives the illusion of control, but it's just an illusion. As you go through your negotiation, don't get too caught up in the details and choices. Your goal here is to focus on "getting to possible" right now, knowing that it all may change as your life unfolds. We'll cover managing change in the next chapter.

How do you "get to possible"? In my practice I use a fancy-sounding tool called "stochastic modeling," or "Monte Carlo simulations." There are plenty of these tools out there that you can play with. A word of caution, however: The assumptions within them vary widely, which can drastically impact results.

Monte Carlo simulations allow you to plug in different numbers and see the likely result. They can help you see the possibility of achieving any number of goal packages from the variables outlined above. You can then dial up or down any of the elements and see how that affects the whole. Monte Carlo simulations also take into account both positive and negative uncertainty in the markets.

The output of a "Monte" is a percentage confidence ratio of success in achieving the stated goals. I generally look for a confidence rate of about 85 percent. Rather nonintuitively, you don't want to be too high in your confidence rate; higher is not better. The reason is that it sacrifices today for tomorrow. It sacrifices the only life you have for fictitious uncertainty. If your scenario rates a very high confidence level, your teeter-totter is leaning too far in one direction; you've negotiated away too much of your current life. Or you're not asking enough out of retirement.

After we plug in all the numbers into the Monte Carlo engine, you may find your ideal retirement in every category is possible. Awesome. Go for it. If you find it's not, it's time to negotiate. The good news is that everything's on the table. Nothing was sidelined without being examined. It's time to find out what's most important and make it happen.

Let's say you're fifty-five and you're wondering if the ideal retirement you've dreamed up is possible:

- Retire at age sixty
- $1,500,000 in investment assets
- $30,000 annual savings rate
- $100,000 lifestyle budget during retirement
- $10,000 annual travel for fifteen years
- $400,000 retirement home purchase at age sixty-five
- $1,000,000 estate at your death
- $40,000 consulting income from age sixty to sixty-five
- $24,500 Social Security starting at age sixty-six
- A portfolio with a targeted maximum loss annually of −17 percent

If you run your ideal scenario and discover it isn't possible, you need to negotiate with yourself. This can be one of those messy meetings because generally a client and I will renegotiate multiple times, testing each scenario to see how it sits with him or her. Through this process and the discussions that take place, he or she slowly discovers not only what's important to him/her, but what's important to the spouse as well.

From the list above, what items are most important to you? Are the retirement date, lifestyle, and travel budgets must-haves? No problem, you dial down other life goals until you find your possible. Perhaps you have to give up 50 percent of your $1,000,000 estate goal and take a bit more investment risk to achieve your possible. Or maybe that retirement home was just an aspiration, so you eliminate it and realize you could easily earn $60,000 consulting. Your must-haves may be different than that of another person who is facing an identical negotiation. Others may feel strongly about leaving the $1,000,000 estate and not taking more investment risk. In this scenario, the negotiation and outcome would be completely different. The ultimate solution will be unique for each unique family.

I've had this happen many times in my years walking life with clients. Once in the late 1990s, I had two clients who were identical on paper. Both were engineers for the same company, were roughly the same age, were married with one child, and had similar incomes and net worth. Very quickly, their net worth went from normal to well over $10 million as the result of an IPO. Because they were so similar, a paint-by-numbers planning process would have created almost identical solutions for them, but when I talked to them, it turned out their goals were very different.

Jimmy wanted to own a jet and become a titan of industry. Jimmy was "all in" at the company. He believed it would continue to do well, and he was very hesitant to capture any paper wealth to better his current financial situation. He believed his shares would ultimately make him super rich. Based on his goals, we created a plan to capture enough "don't go broke" money by selling shares over a three-year period, and let the rest ride with the fortunes of the firm.

Sam, on the other hand, was much more conservative. Although he believed in the company, he was much more concerned about his family's financial security. His deal-breaker was "I am not working a lick past sixty." Sam's plan called for the sale of enough shares to secure his priority of retiring at sixty and being financially secure.

Jimmy's and Sam's plans called for different sacrifices in different areas. Jimmy risked more volatility in order to achieve something for which he cared more. Sam risked greater possible lifestyle opportunities in order to buy himself confidence that he could retire at age sixty. In both cases, the plan developed was right for them.

Wondering how their plans worked out? Well, the company didn't prosper and now no longer exists. Jimmy, although he didn't get his jet, is a titan of industry of sorts and is doing well. His priorities have changed drastically over the last decade, and he now has a completely different plan. Sam was able to secure his retirement but still works. Turns out, retiring at sixty didn't suit him. He now can't see himself retiring, and works—on his own terms— and is loving life.

LIVING IN THE NOW

Just like Jimmy and Sam, your negotiated "possible" won't work out as planned. That's OK. In fact, it's never meant to. The negotiation and Monte Carlo simulations are not trying to predict the future. We're comfortable not knowing. We know we can never have certainty about the future. Instead, they give us data so we can act to create a great life, rather than simply react. They allow us to be nimble and squeeze as much out of our life as possible now and in the future.

When you're considering negotiation and going through the process, you want to live well right now and be confident about tomorrow (remember that teeter-totter?). The process helps you find answers to the most important questions about retiring:

What lifestyle could I live?

Will I run out of money?

Can I do _____?

Is _____ reasonable?

Can we afford _____ without putting our future in jeopardy?

Can I save less to live better now?

Am I taking too much/too little investment risk?

You're planning for the future, but tomorrow is promised to no one. Look around at your family, friends, and community, and you'll see that life can be very short. Make sure you live your life while you're healthy enough to do so. Never forget to live in the present while planning for the future.

CHAPTER SUMMARY

☐ **Negotiation—Inside the Lines**—If you stay inside the lines of the paint-by-numbers approach, you'll probably not like the negotiation. It sees your art (life) as a basic math problem. If their math says you can't reach your goals, the solutions are limited.

☐ **Negotiation—Outside the Lines**—Living outside the lines can help you think more creatively about your life and focus on achieving the things you care about most.

☐ **Getting to Possible**—There are no guarantees in life, so it's best to focus on what is possible rather than trying to find guarantees. This dynamic approach allows you to confidently act and make adjustments as your life unfolds.

CHAPTER 9
START YOUR JOURNEY

"A great retirement comes from having the right little conversations about life and money."

—ROGER WHITNEY

Starting your journey is much easier than many think. After thinking about life and your future, it can be easy to get bogged down. It all seems so far away. It also seems like such a big task that anything you do today will hardly put a dent in the journey. A great life is built one moment at a time. Just as Dorothy went down the yellow brick road one ruby-slippered step at a time, you'll create your great life that way too... one step at a time (ruby slippers optional).

STAY LIGHT ON YOUR FEET

Look too far ahead, and you're likely to stumble and even fall down. As your life unfolds, you'll need to stay light on your feet so you can adjust quickly. Unlike climbing a mountain with a fixed peak, your destination will likely change direction many times. Health, relationships, the economy, and markets can throw your plans off course. These are virtually impossible to predict. You'll need to have a system to identify issues and adjust quickly. Another reason, not as easily identified, is that YOU will change over time. The things you enjoy, value, and aspire to will evolve. As you change, so will your journey; it makes sense to focus on getting each step right, rather than plotting out the entire route.

If you're married, you'll have two sets of priorities to stay in tune with (yours and your spouse's). As my wife and I walk life together, we continue to change. When we acknowledge this truth and lean into it, we plan more dynamically.

You're not following a predetermined blueprint; you're building your life, your masterpiece. You can't let yourself get trapped by what is. Your life is ever-evolving and your plan should be too. Even artists like Picasso changed direction often. X-rays of his masterpiece *The Old Guitarist* revealed two failed attempts. If a master artist can adjust course when his passion shifts, so can you.

In many ways, this outside-the-lines approach releases you from getting it right the first time. If you set a course for a beautiful future life, you're allowed to abandon it for an even better one if that comes along. The outside-the-lines approach will help keep you from being overwhelmed. If you see retirement goals as absolutes, reality hits. A goal is something that has to be achieved or you're a failure. It's easy to get overwhelmed, because it's too much to figure out. Whether we're talking about inflation, the markets, health, relationships, work, or income, it's impossible to effectively plan for the next twenty to thirty years. Embrace the uncertainty. Your plans are going to change either by your design or life circumstances.

I was talking with a gentleman the other day who's sixty-five. His wife is retired. He was planning on retiring when he was sixty-eight, but he's seeing changes in his wife's behavior that concern him. She has diabetes and has managed it forever, but lately she's forgetting things. Something is going on. He's worried she'll not be as active in three more years. Although this isn't what he'd envisioned, he's rethinking his plan on working three more years. Their goals are going to evolve to assure they make more of their time now, while she's still well.

The opposite can happen. You could find yourself in a situation where you really hit your stride in those last five years of work. Maybe you make great money, find that you're going to be able to do consulting totally on your own terms, or inherit a significant amount. You may be able to do things that you never thought you'd be able to do. Again, your aspirations and dreams will evolve.

Pivot or alter your course as aspirations and circumstances change. Write long-term aspirations in pencil and plan on evolving as life does. This will keep you from being overwhelmed when life happens, for the good or the bad. It will keep you from freezing or making rash decisions and, most importantly, it will keep you from being susceptible to "gurus" who promise false solutions to salve your fear.

TALK WHILE YOU WALK: THE SECRET TO A GOOD MARRIAGE

"Well, that's just great!" you say. "How am I supposed to manage my life and finances if my life is going to 'evolve' constantly?" It might seem frustrating, but it's actually a great thing and much easier to manage than figuring it all out. The secret is avoiding BIG conversations.

I often ask new clients the secret to a good marriage. I get lots of different answers: communication, always saying "yes, Dear," a great love life, common hobbies; it runs the gamut. All are great answers, but I'm much more pragmatic than that. My secret to a good marriage is that I never want to have a BIG conversation with my wife. I've had BIG conversations with my wife, and they're no fun for anyone. They typically happen when we've failed to have the little conversations to stay in sync. The best way to do that is to make sure we're talking as we walk through life together.

Here's a big-conversation scenario: A husband and wife have a conversation about where they're going to live in retirement. They agree, "We're in our forever home. We're going to pay it off, stay here, and are never going to move." They start walking hand in hand with that vision. As their life unfolds, their daughter graduates from college, strikes out on her own, and moves three states away. A few years later she marries a wonderful guy, and then they have a child. The first grandbaby! The wife spends more and more time flying out to visit, and in her mind, starts to live a different life. She begins to think, *I've got to be near my grandbaby. Maybe we should move there.* Meanwhile, the husband is still working, and he's thinking about the workshop he'll build in "our forever home." This is a simple and typical example, but it could be either spouse and it could be anything. Dreams and aspirations change, but if one spouse never really informs the other one, when that retirement day arrives, there's a big problem. The wife says, "We're selling this house and moving," and a BIG conversation takes place. You don't want one of those. Trust me; I've seen them . . . *no fun.*

In my twenty-five years of working with clients, I've unfortunately had to bear witness to many divorces—nasty ones, sad ones, and everything in between. Many times couples don't know what sparked it. They say they grew apart, they don't love each other anymore, or there was an affair, but at the core is a feeling of not being connected. There's often not one big event, but the lack of all the little conversations over the years that results in their growing apart, and eventual divorce or hard road back to happiness.

If we live inside our head and don't stay in tune with how our aspirations are developing and then communicate those developments to the important people in our lives, the resulting big conversation can be potentially devastating, both personally and financially. It seems so simple, but little conversations can be hard to have.

BIG conversations can occur outside of our head as well. One of the hardest parts of managing assets is knowing when it's time to make a little adjustment to spending, saving, investing, or another item, in order to stay on track.

Some of the saddest BIG conversations I've been part of were in the aftermath of the bursting of the tech bubble in 2000 and the Great Recession of 2007–2009. The 1990s were a great decade for US stocks, especially technology companies. It was in the dot-com bubble where nearly everything related to the Internet went up—a lot—and everything unrelated to it didn't. The NASDAQ–100 (a technology-heavy weighted index during the 1990s) experienced an average return between 1991 and 1999 of 38 percent per year (NASDAQ 2017). By the end of the decade, investing seemed easy, and I saw many people retire assuming they could "conservatively" earn 20 percent per year on their investments and safely withdraw 10 percent or more to live on. In fact, many "experts" touted the benefits of the new economy and advised investing 100 percent in stocks and just selling when you needed spending money.

When the dot-com bubble burst in 2000 and the NASDAQ–100 lost 57 percent of its value in three years (2000–2002), there were a lot of BIG conversations taking place. I recall one I had in 2001 with a gentleman who had retired in 1998 with a plan to take $120,000 from his $1,000,000 portfolio. It worked for the first few years; then, as the dot-com bubble burst, his losses started to mount. Rather than have a little conversation and adjust course, he continued on—and the losses mounted. By the time he walked into my office, his portfolio was decimated. He knew he had to go back to work, but had few options after being out of the work force for three and a half years.

A similar story played out in the aftermath of the Great Recession of 2007–2009. This time, a real estate bubble sparked the downturn, but unlike in 2000, when it was primarily technology companies that suffered, in 2008, virtually every asset got caught up in the downturn. BIG conversations didn't happen because of bad assumptions (like in 2001). They happened because many followed inside-the-lines advice that perfectly positioned them to experience their maximum tolerance for volatility, whether they needed it or not.

The main reason we let things escalate to BIG conversations is we're busy leading a life full of urgent, but not crucially important, things. If you're like me, when you get home, you just want to enjoy life, family, pets, hobbies, and friends. Avoiding little issues helps keep things humming along. *Best to let it go* or *It'll get better,* you say to yourself. The timing never seems right. However, you have to have little sometimes-uncomfortable conversations to avoid BIG potentially devastating ones.

THE LITTLE CONVERSATIONS

There are four little conversations I suggest you have on a regular basis. Each addresses a different area of your financial life. Establish a natural rhythm of having them, and you'll be able to identify and make little adjustments as your life unfolds. Unlike typical financial conversations, these shouldn't get bogged down in the past or focus too far out into the future. The key word is "little." Once you've gone through the process, each of these should be easy to do. They're meant to help you keep your priorities clear and be intentional about steps you can take today to make a better life. Let's briefly outline each little conversation and how often you should have them.

1. Goals and Aspirations

Once a year, have an in-depth discussion about your goals and aspirations. Discuss what you'd like your life to be like in the coming year, and examine the needs, wants, and wishes you've set previously. Be careful not to get trapped by previous plans. Just because they were important to you last year, doesn't mean they still are. Each day, you have the chance to start anew. As you review your past priorities, make them stand up now.

Are they still relevant? If so, do they need to be adjusted? In my business, clients are constantly adjusting their goals and aspirations to align with their priorities. Each day gives you more information about your future. Use this to calibrate your course. If past goals are no longer relevant, scrap them. Crumple them up and start over. It's not uncommon to have completely new priorities every year or so. Go back and create an entirely new set of needs, wants, and wishes.

In fact, this is a great exercise to do every now and then. Like a train, it's easy to start down a track and never get off. Unlike a train, you can lay a new course whenever you want. Starting from scratch now and again can help refresh your thinking.

2. Cash Flow

Every month, have a little conversation to review your cash flow. Doing so will help you stay abreast of the financial health of the household and stay connected. I suggest you not make this the dreaded budget meeting. Instead, make it fun. Yup, you heard right, I said make it fun. Get out of your normal environment. Instead of having it at the kitchen table, go to a quiet restaurant or coffee shop (if you're married, have a date afterward). This conversation is best done looking forward for risks and opportunities (not looking backward).

Questions to address could include:

- What income did we have for the month?
- What do we expect in the coming months?
- What are risk and opportunities for our income?
- What were our lifestyle expenses for the month?
- What were extraordinary expenses for the month?
- What extraordinary expenses do we expect in the coming months?

3. Net Worth

Every six months, update your net worth statement and, if you have access to it, check your confidence ratio using Monte Carlo software, as we discussed in the last chapter. Use your net worth statement to track the financial progress you've made and decide how best to allocate savings and your other assets to work toward your goals and aspirations. Things to review include:

- Emergency fund
- Savings fund for upcoming extra expenses
- Investment assets (taxable, tax-deferred, and tax-free)
- Use assets
- Debt levels

During each net worth conversation, determine what, if any, adjustments you need to make to the amounts in each bucket. For example, a common one is allocating the savings you've accumulated in your savings account. If you're a good saver, you risk having too much idle money sitting around in a checking or savings account. This is the little conversation to determine how to put it to use. Once you've funded your emergency and extras fund, paid down bad debt (credit cards, etc.), the remainder should either be spent, gifted, or allocated to long-term investment.

Some challenging questions to ask as you review your net worth statement include:

- How big should my emergency fund be?

- What upcoming expenses do I need to plan for?

- Am I paying too much interest on my debt?

- Is my after-tax, pre-tax, and tax-free mix correct?

- Are my investment allocations and vehicles appropriate?

- What are the risks and opportunities?

4. Risk Management

Ahhh, if the first three conversations weren't fun enough, once every two years, you get to evaluate the risks you face in life. This little conversation accomplishes three things. First, it helps you identify potential risks that could derail your life or plan. Home fire, auto accident, major medical event, long-term–care event, and premature death are all examples of risks that most of us face. Second, it helps you quantify each risk and stress test your plan against it. And finally, it helps you determine how much risk, if any, you want to transfer to someone else. By this, I mean an insurance company. Common items to review in your risk conversation are:

- Home insurance needs

- Auto insurance needs

- Umbrella insurance needs

- Life insurance needs

- Long-term–care insurance needs

- Disability insurance needs

Challenging questions include:

- What is the financial risk?
- Can I afford to self-insure?
- If not, how much of the risk can I affordably transfer?
- What are the coverage, limits, and premium for my _____ insurance?

WHERE THESE CONVERSATIONS WILL LEAD YOU

What freaks us out about the future is the not knowing. It's uncomfortable, but having little conversations helps keep you on track and allows you calibrate your retirement flight plan. Your spending, income, and priorities will be different every year or so. You may have health issues, job changes, or personal loss. The market may have done better or worse than you planned. Reviewing the simulations and gauging them against reality is your early warning system.

If you have good fortune or good markets, you can use the result of these tools to proactively make decisions. If you have three good years because things are trending, you'll want to constantly be moving risk down, or perhaps spending a little bit more while the sun is shining. You could plan on leaving a bigger estate, slowing down your work, or take an investment risk to get back down to an 85 percent confidence rate.

On the flip side, what if you have worse-than-expected markets? Some of the big questions that freak out everybody are, "When do I sell? When do I just get out of the way of bad markets?" And, "When do I need to adjust my life because of bad markets?" With no plan or a one-dimensional "fix it and forget it plan," you don't really have a lot of perspective and end up making decisions intuitively based on your fear gauge. Sometimes you make them at exactly the wrong time and give up life that you don't necessarily need to forgo.

When deciding to sell or move on during a really bad market, you have the same conversation as you would in a good market, but in reverse. If your confidence level is at eighty-five but it gets down to a level of seventy-five or below, you know you need to discuss it. What do you need to do to tweak the confidence level back up? Perhaps you change your investment-risk level this year until things improve. You might allow cash reserves to drain a bit rather than pull from the portfolio and sell at the wrong time. Perhaps you work a little bit and earn the money for the trip rather than taking it from your assets. All of these things will move that confidence percentage back up and keep you from an asset fire sale.

If you go through an '07 or '08 experience, where there is bad market after bad market after bad market, you'll have little adjustment after little adjustment after little adjustment. That really will help you to be proactive in making choices to protect your assets, not just now but in the future. When things turn around, it will make it that much easier to start moving in a positive direction using the assets preserved in the down market.

Most of us don't know when we need to get out of the market, as there is no perspective and no framework for grappling with that decision, and what we hear in the media can skew our vision. I've had plenty of instances in which there was a huge market correction, and when I reran the simulations, the client was still in the low eighties. That works. The client didn't have to do a thing. It was a scary time, but looking at it objectively gave perspective. The client was fine on the current timeline.

Retirement planning isn't solely wealth maximization; it's *life* maximization. As an investment professional, when we go through really stressful markets, like the beginning of 2016, before I even talk to my clients, I rerun the Monte Carlo simulations to see how the market has affected the confidence level of achieving their goals. Cooler heads can prevail.

YOUR JOURNEY MIGHT LEAD TO A TRAILER

You've accepted the uncertainty that comes in life. When you plan for the rhythms and seasons of life, you don't know what's going to happen in the future. If you can't predict the future, you shouldn't spend any time trying to do so. You just need to make some reasonable assumptions and have a really good process to help you make the right decisions along the way, while staying as flexible as possible. You can thoughtfully navigate your way to the best result.

The key is a system that quickly triggers course corrections. You don't want your plan to have time to stray too far off course. Trust yourself and your system to identify where the corrections need to be made to mitigate the loss and damage. You don't have to try to figure out the next twenty or thirty years or the entire course of your retirement, you just have to be willing to have the little conversations and to be OK with the unknown. This isn't a "fix it and forget it" situation.

When I walk through planning with clients, I tell them, "We're going to execute on this. We're going to be faithful, and we're going to work on having those little conversations so we can make adjustments. You do realize that this may not prevent you from having to live in a run-down trailer when you're older?" They look at me like, *What?!? What are you talking about? Then why are we doing this?*

The reason is because we can't control the future. It's possible that everything in your life could go wrong: health, relationships, work, and money. It's a very unlikely possibility, but you have to account for the fact that lots of things could go wrong. The market and economy could start on a free fall and never recover. The doomsday scenarios could come true. Everything could align to create the perfect storm. What could you do if that happens? The answer is: Manage through the storm.

If you have a process involving a lot of little conversations, you identify the possibilities and use the conversations to mitigate the damage as quickly as possible. You stay on course by making lots and lots of little changes along the way. Even if you end up living in a little trailer down by the river, if you are prudent, if you are diligent in having the little conversations and making lots of little adjustments, you'll be one of the last people moving into a trailer. You'll know it's coming and will be maximizing your life then and for the future.

You won't go from your nice, comfortable suburban house directly to the trailer. That's what happens when people don't pay attention. They let things get out of hand, and they don't make adjustments early. They have huge conversations: "Honey we're selling the BMW and the house, and moving into an apartment." When you don't pay attention, you have no options.

> # Go to rockretirementbook.com for a "little conversation" checklist.

EVERY NOW AND THEN, DO A S.M.A.R.T. SPRINT

PERSONAL

PROFESSIONAL

FINANCIAL

As you have these little conversations, you'll discover opportunities to speed up your journey toward a great life. By being intentional and directing the course of your life rather than just letting life happen, you'll be amazed at what you discover. When you find these opportunities, use what I call a "S.M.A.R.T. Sprint." These are short bursts of energy in particular areas of your life designed to accomplish short-term goals that align with long-term goals. Let's break down how a S.M.A.R.T. Sprint works.

There are three key elements to a S.M.A.R.T. Sprint. First, there's S.M.A.R.T., an acronym used in goal setting that stands for:

Specific

Measurable

Actionable

Realistic

Time-bound

For example, "I need to exercise more this year" is not a goal that is S.M.A.R.T. A S.M.A.R.T. goal would be, "[By X date], I feel great and have more energy because I've been walking for twenty minutes at least four days per week." Notice it doesn't read, "I will . . ." It's stated as a fact, not an aspiration. It also has incorporated how you feel when you're taking the twenty-minute walks. These are subtle, but important, differences.

Second is "Sprint." Sprint is, well, a sprint. A short burst of energy focused on a specific objective. I suggest your sprint last between sixty and ninety days. You want it short enough that it's within reach with focused attention, but long enough so you can develop better habits. The further out the goal, the less urgency to it. Back in school, did you study for the test a month ahead of time or the day before the exam? Short goals demand your attention; that's the beauty of a sprint.

Finally, attach a reward to it. The bigger the sprint, the bigger the reward. Celebrate each step you take along the way. In fact, don't simply attach the reward; set it up to occur. For example, recently I set a big ninety-day goal to come to agreement on an important business deal. My reward was to spend a weekend with my wife at a local resort. The day I set the goal, I booked the room and informed my wife of my intent. Talk about motivation. It *had* to happen!

Let's look at some of the areas in which you can set S.M.A.R.T. Sprints, and what impact that could have on your life. Following are some of my favorite areas.

> **You can visit rockretirementbook.com for a "S.M.A.R.T. Sprint" worksheet to set your own Sprint.**

Personal S.M.A.R.T. Sprint

Personal growth is a key ingredient in a retirement masterpiece. Personal growth includes your physical, mental, and intellectual health, as well as the health of your family and friend relationships. These affect every other area of your life. This is where real happiness originates. We often try to improve our personal life with hollow New Year's resolutions like "I'm going to start exercising this year." That's an admirable goal, but often it's over in a just a few weeks.

If physical health is the area you want to focus on, a S.M.A.R.T. Sprint would be like the one just mentioned, "By [X date], I feel great and have more energy because I've been walking for twenty minutes at least four days per week." That's a specific, measurable, actionable, realistic, and time-bound goal—not too big to intimidate or too small to matter. Then, as a reward, go eat a piece of cake . . . or no, don't do that. :-)

Another area where you can set a personal S.M.A.R.T. Sprint is in your marriage. A year ago, I set a personal S.M.A.R.T. Sprint to send my wife and two children an email or a handwritten note once a week telling them something I appreciate or admire about them. I didn't set a goal to "spend more time with my kids" because I know that doesn't work. My goal for this Sprint was twofold. First, I wanted to infuse good thoughts into their hearts to help them live better. Second, I wanted to cultivate my spirit of thankfulness. My reward? It was witnessing their reactions as they went from a simple "Thanks" to a roll of the eyes (there goes Dad again) to hugs and warm conversations.

Too mushy for you? Consider the costs of not developing rich relationships. One element of your personal life that changes as you get older is loneliness. A S.M.A.R.T. Sprint to counteract the loss of friends is to contact one acquaintance a week and invite him or her out for a drink. You could also join a group at church and go every week for the next six months. A personal S.M.A.R.T. Sprint that encompasses both physical health and friendship is arriving at the gym ten minutes before class and chatting with the people next to you.

When you accomplish an aspiration, reward yourself. Whether it's playing Xbox or playing a game on your iPhone, you get badges, you reach new secret levels, or you receive new weapons. S.M.A.R.T. Sprints are the gamification of life. You have these sprints so you can always be working toward something very specific, something you can go out and accomplish, leading you toward building a beautiful life.

Professional S.M.A.R.T. Sprint

The second area ripe for S.M.A.R.T. Sprints is your professional life. As I've mentioned throughout this book, progress in this area could be the jet fuel to launch you toward your ideal retirement. How do you earn more money to live better today and tomorrow? How do you position yourself better financially? Being frugal only takes you so far. A S.M.A.R.T. Sprint isn't, "I need to network more" or "I should think about learning a new skill." A S.M.A.R.T. Sprint to build relationships vertically could be, "By [X date], I have more confidence in my career, because I have met with four division heads within my company." Or "By [X date], I feel more confident and informed, because I have met with three thought leaders in my industry." A S.M.A.R.T. Sprint could be, "By [X date], am a key team member because I'm an expert at [X]." These types of S.M.A.R.T. Sprints done religiously will bring you opportunities for advancement and growth that you would never have otherwise. They will also help you in Step Three: The Income Impact, work after retirement.

Whether it's increasing your knowledge or your network, you can build your career and income using S.M.A.R.T. Sprints. Everyone, even those not in the job market, can set a professional goal. It could be learning a skill set, like the woman who sews flags, or learning a language. In retirement, you can hone a skill or hobby. You can sharpen yourself as a person instead of just letting the years flow by.

Financial S.M.A.R.T. Sprint

You can write these S.M.A.R.T. Sprints yourself now. "By [X date], I feel more secure because I no longer owe [X amount] of debt" or

"By [X date], I've consolidated my investments and implemented a well-thought-out asset allocation so that I am confident about my financial future." You can set very specific goals focused on your spending, savings, investing, or debt reduction. Your net worth statement doesn't go from negative to multimillion dollars at once; it gets there inch by inch. Setting S.M.A.R.T. Sprints helps you get those quick wins and move the ball forward. "I need to have an emergency fund," is a dream, a wish. "By [X date], I feel amazing because I have [X amount] in my emergency fund" is a great goal. Adjust the sprints in your life as your aspirations and dreams unfold, and you will navigate your way to a great life.

The Reward

Don't forget the reward! Whatever S.M.A.R.T. Sprint your family accomplishes, celebrate it. Make it a big deal. Make talking about and planning for the future a fun sport. Teach your kids that money and planning isn't boring, but a means to work toward an incredible life and retirement. If you're single, create a group of like-minded friends to support each other's effort and celebrate successes. If you're married, the personal and professional S.M.A.R.T. Sprints are individual, but the financial one should be set together. As you engage in these little conversations, pick a reward to celebrate the accomplishment. Of course, accomplishing the S.M.A.R.T. Sprint is a reward itself because you have a better personal, professional, and financial life, but rewarding yourself ties what you want in the short term with what you want in the long term. When you write down your S.M.A.R.T. Sprints, outline the reward at the bottom and then track the Sprint together with your spouse or friends and celebrate.

Many of my clients have established weekly date nights and use the time to enjoy each other and track how they're doing. They have wine and just talk about the week. It's an accountability date where they support each other in their goals and see how they are progressing. They cheer each other on, asking, "Where do you need help?" and "Where are you stuck?" When one of them achieves something, they don't go to their regular place, they do something special, such as an overnight stay with a visit to a much nicer restaurant they've been wanting to try, and then they set the next S.M.A.R.T. Sprint.

YOU HAVE THE POWER

You can thrive outside the lines. You can create your own path, using your smarts, imagination, and ability to apply steady effort toward your ideal life. Having lots of little conversations about the right things and setting S.M.A.R.T. Sprints focused on taking the next step are all things YOU can control. They're things YOU can make happen, regardless of the world around you. To paraphrase one of my favorite childhood cartoon heroes, He-Man (and She-Ra), "YOU HAVE THE POWER!" Now go use it!

Go to rockretirementbook.com for checklists to help you have each of the little conversations.

CHAPTER SUMMARY

☐ **Stay Light on Your Feet**—Life is change. Many aspects of it are unknowable. Once you dream up your masterpiece and start creating it, it's OK to change it as your life unfolds.

☐ **Talk While You Walk**—Have the right little conversations along your journey to identify changes, adjust your course, and make the most of how your life unfolds.

☐ **The Little Conversations**—There are four little conversations I suggest you have on a regular basis. Each addresses a different area of your financial life. Establish a natural rhythm of having them, and you'll be able to identify them and make little adjustments as your life unfolds.

☐ **Do S.M.A.R.T. Sprints**—Each year, set S.M.A.R.T. Sprints in your personal, professional, and financial lives.

CHAPTER 10
GO CREATE
A GREAT LIFE

"You have brains in your head. You have feet
in your shoes. You can steer yourself any direction
you choose. You're on your own. And you know
what you know. And YOU are the one
who'll decide where to go . . . "

—DR. SEUSS, *OH, THE PLACES YOU'LL GO!*

Life is what happens while you are making other plans." I've witnessed this sentiment from John Lennon up close. Life happened to my mom as she sacrificed her life for a tomorrow that never came. Life happened to many who sacrificed too much of their today only to realize they could have sacrificed less and lived more. Life eventually happened to many who enjoyed too much of today and were left with only undesirable choices in retirement.

Life will happen to you.

The question is whether or not you will walk with purpose in creating a life you want. Will you balance your seesaw between living well today and securing your tomorrow? Will you be awake at the wheel to adjust as your life unfolds?

A WORD OF CAUTION

When it comes to planning for the future, there's a tendency to take things that are important, but not urgent, and put them on the back burner. With dual-income families, kids, serving the community, and everything else, we're just running so hard. There have been reams written about how little margin we have and how short our attention spans have become. We're caught on a treadmill of stuff. When I get home, I've got to work out, skim the pool, replace a lightbulb, wash the dishes, respond to email messages, finish a project; there are so many things to do and they never stop arriving.

The really important things never feel urgent, so they get put off. They could be planning for retirement, doing things with your children, having date night with your spouse, taking care of your estate plan, paying down that debt, starting a 401(k), managing your investments, or tracking spending. We know these things are important, but we never seem to get around to them.

In my practice, I've found people delve into the important, but not urgent, things when there's some kind of pressure point. For example, when someone in their circle of friends passes away unexpectedly, it brings things like life insurance, estate planning, or spending time with family to the forefront. There's a little window of time when the iron is hot. You come out of the matrix, sort of like Neo did, and see the world in a new way. If you don't strike and take care of that important thing when it feels urgent, the urgency will pass. You'll fall back into the rhythm of the routine. You are at such a juncture right now. You've read this book, and it's caused you to think. The iron is hot now. Now is the time for action.

FIVE REGRETS TO AVOID

Bronnie Ware is a hospice nurse in Australia who wrote a best-selling book, *The Top Five Regrets of the Dying.* These are basically a mirror, us looking back and speaking to ourselves from near to the grave. When I read her book, it hit me. This could be me when I'm eighty or ninety and looking back at my life. If I'm not intentional about my life, when I'm on my deathbed, these are the things I might say. My hope for you is that by having the little conversations that matter, you'll avoid having these regrets too.

1. I wish I'd had the courage to live a life true to myself, not the life others expected of me.

Everyone has roles created for them based on the people around them: parents, superiors, and/or coworkers. People are husbands, wives, fathers, mothers, employees, employer, etc. Seeking approval from those around them, knowingly or perhaps unknowingly, dictates who people become. People create lives based on others' rules and expectations. Perhaps a man is in a business that's not aligned with his ideals any longer, but he has a role he's created that, frankly, he's successful in. But as he has matured and changed, it's not a fit anymore; it's not reflective of his true self.

Try something: Go to a quiet place and sit, eyes closed. Breathe deeply for one minute; now imagine yourself at age ninety sitting in a rocking chair on a porch on a beautiful fall day. Now say aloud, "I wish I'd had the courage to live a life true to myself." How would it make you feel if you were sitting there, realizing you'd lived your life based on others' expectations? This doesn't have to be your reality. You can discover what your true self wants. Dream up your ideal retirement without the baggage of the past clouding your vision. Create a vision for what will be and start walking toward it. Have the little conversations that matter to adjust as your life unfolds.

2. I wish I hadn't worked so hard.

On his or her deathbed no one ever said, "Gee, I wish I had spent more time in the office, on the computer, in meetings, traveling for work, etc." Bronnie Ware says every single male patient, and many of the women, voiced this regret.

Work gives us an easy outlet to avoid personal depth in our life. It's easy to fool ourselves and say we work so hard to meet our obligations. This is true . . . to a point. But in my experience, even when someone reaches "financial independence," the pace of work doesn't slow. It often intensifies because there are now more responsibilities and obligations. Success is addictive—so addictive, it's easy to use it to escape building deeper relationships with those who are truly important to us.

3. I wish I'd had the courage to express my feelings.

It's easy not having the little conversations that matter. It can be scary telling someone, "I love you," "I'm sorry," or "I'm afraid." I'm not sure why it's so hard, but it just is. For years, I had difficulty telling my wife these things. I felt them; I just couldn't say them. I think she felt the same way. As a result, our relationship was like a silent dance moving between closeness and separateness. Once we matured and opened up, our relationship blossomed. By not expressing your feelings, you lose your voice. You're not truly yourself.

4. I wish I had stayed in touch with my friends.

We can create a great financial plan for an amazing retirement, but staying connected and investing in relationships is what colors in the spaces inside the lines. Relationships are the crayons that make it come alive.

5. I wish that I had let myself be happier.

This one really hit me personally. I wish I had forgiven myself earlier for past mistakes. Allowing those things to fester muted my happiness. Forgiving myself released my past mistakes and allowed me to look forward to what could be.

If you're over forty, you have screwed up a lot. I can remember making lots of money in my twenties and thinking it would never end. I did everything wrong and didn't save much—and I was a financial planner! I spent all of my thirties trying to clean up the mess and was really angry with myself for how stupid I had been. It really affected my happiness, but more importantly, it affected the happiness of my wife and children because I was a jerk to them in a lot of ways. All of this stemmed from not forgiving myself for my financial mistakes. I know I'm not alone in failing to give myself grace.

If you were being nursed by Bronnie right now, you'd likely have some or all of these regrets—but you are where you are.

You can't go backward any more than you could if you were on your deathbed, but you can go forward. Don't try to correct what happened or beat yourself up; instead be intentional about how you live your life from this moment forward in all the areas that we've talked about in the book.

You are the pioneer in this grand experiment of painting your retirement masterpiece. The paint-by-numbers approach your parents used won't work for you. You won't settle for collecting bond interest while you stop by the library and hit the early-bird special for dinner. Sitting on the park bench of life won't cut it. Retirement for you is about getting out on the playground; it's about pursuing passions, adventure, and relationships you've only been able to touch the surface of during your working years. Your retirement requires a new approach, an exciting one, one you direct.

This new frontier may sound a bit intimidating. You might say, "I don't want to be the pioneer! Why can't someone else just have all the answers?" I get it. The unknown can be scary. Stop looking for answers. Stop trying to eliminate uncertainty. Stop grasping onto gurus who say they have the answers. Instead, lean into the experience. Accept what you know (and don't know), dream up an ideal retirement, and take it one step at a time, adjusting along the way. "Oh the places you'll go!"

RESOURCES

For a list of worksheets mentioned throughout the book,

as well as other helpful financial tips,

please visit rockretirementbook.com.

ABOUT THE AUTHOR

Roger Whitney is a cofounder of WWK Wealth Advisors and host of the award-winning podcast *The Retirement Answer Man.* He has been a financial advisor for over twenty-five years. Each day he "walks life" with individuals and families, helping them plan for, transition into, and live out their retirement.

He is a former instructor of retirement planning and employee benefits for the Certified Financial Planner® certificate program at the University of Texas at Arlington. He has also taught wealth management at Texas Christian University Extended Education.

Certifications include:

- Certified Financial Planner (CFP®), CFP Board of Standards

- Certified Investment Management Analyst CIMA®), in conjunction with the Wharton School through the Investment Management Consultant's Association.

- Certified Private Wealth Advisor (CPWA®), Chartered Private Wealth Advisor®, awarded at University of Chicago Booth School of Business

- Accredited Investment Fiduciary (AIF®), conduction with the Center for Fiduciary Studies and Fi360

He lives in the Fort Worth, Texas, area with his wife, Shauna, and two children.

REFERENCES

Atalanta Sosnoff Capital. 2016. http://www.atalantasosnoff.com/

Braveheart. Directed by Mel Gibson. 1995. Los Angeles: Paramount Pictures Home Entertainment, 2013. Blu-ray.

CFP Board. 2017. "Financial Planning Practice Standards." Accessed January 17.

http://www.cfp.net/for-cfp-professionals/professional-standards-enforcement/standards-of-professional-conduct/financial-planning-practice-standards.

Corbin, Kenneth. "Boomers' Retirement Confidence Hits All-Time Low." *Financial Planning,*

April 13, 2016. http://www.financial-planning.com/news/boomers-retirement-confidence-hits-all-time-low.

Dilworth, Kelly. "Average credit card interest rate increases to 14.9 percent." *Creditcards.com,* March 25, 2015. http://www.creditcards.com/credit-card-news/interest-rate-report-032515-up-2121.php

El Issa, Erin. 2016. "2016 American Household Credit Card Debt Study." *NerdWallet*. https://www.nerdwallet.com/blog/credit-card-data/average-credit-card-debt-household/.

Ferri, Rick. "It's Official! Gurus Can't Accurately Predict Markets." *Forbes,* January 10, 2013. http://www.forbes.com/sites/rickferri/2013/01/10/ts-official-gurus-cant-accurately-predict-markets/#7b27f23218d9

The Investment Company Institute. *The 2014 Investment Company Fact Book: A Review of Trends and Activities in the U.S. Investment Company Industry, 54th edition.* Online edition. https://www.ici.org/pdf/2014_factbook.pdf

Gamble, Kenneth, Leon Huff and Anthony Jackson. *Ship Ahoy.* Philadelphia: Philadelphia International Records,1973.

Gratton, Lynda, and Andrew Scott. *The 100-Year Life — Living and Working in an Age of Longevity.* London: Bloomsbury, 2016.

Intuit QuickBooks Resource Center. "Ready to Start a Business? Here's What It Will Cost." Accessed January 19, 2017. http://quickbooks.intuit.com/r/business-planning/start-costs-industry/.

Investment Company Institute. 2014. "Frequently Asked Questions About 401(k) Plans." Last modified September. https://www.ici.org/policy/retirement/plan/401k/faqs_401k.

Jacobe, Dennis. "One in Three Americans Prepare a Detailed Household Budget." *Gallup,* June 3, 2013. http://www.gallup.com/poll/162872/one-three-americans-prepare-detailed-household-budget.aspx

Johnson, David. "These Charts Show the Baby Boomers Coming Health Crisis." *TIME Magazine,* May 11, 2015. http://time.com/3852306/baby-boomer-health-charts/.

Johnson, Teddi Dinely. "Healthy relationships lead to better lives." *The Nation's Health,* March 2011. http://thenationshealth.aphapublications.org/content/41/2/20.full.

The Karate Kid. Directed by John G. Avildsen. 1984. Culver City: Sony Pictures Home Entertainment, 2010. Blu-ray.

Laguipo, Angela. "Michelangelo Battled Arthritic Hands While Producing Some Of His Masterpieces." *Tech Times,* February 6, 2016. http://www.techtimes.com/articles/131010/20160206/michelangelo-battled-arthritic-hands-while-producing-some-of-his-masterpieces.htm.

Lockard, Pamela. "The Truth About Baby Boomers and Social Media." DMN3, July 1, 2015. http://www.dmn3.com/dmn3-blog/boomers-and-social-media.

Merriam-Webster Dictionary. 2017. Accessed January 19. https://www.merriam-webster.com/

Miller, Mark. 2016. *Career Pivot.* http://careerpivot.com.

National Center for Health Statistics. *Health, United States, 2014: With Special Feature on Adults Aged 55–64.* Hyattsville, MD. 2015. Online edition. https://www.cdc.gov/nchs/data/hus/hus14.pdf

Nasdaq. 2017. "Nasdaq 100." Accessed January 19. http://www.nasdaq.com/markets/indices/nasdaq-100.aspx

New York Stock Exchange. 2017. Accessed January 31. https://www.nyse.com/the-exchange

Pant, Paula. 2016. *Afford Anything.* http://affordanything.com.

Stangler, Dane. "In Search of a Second Act: The Challenges and Advantages of Senior Entrepreneurship." Ewing Marion Kauffman Foundation website, February 12, 2014. http://www.kauffman.org/what-we-do/research/2014/02/the-challenges-and-advantages-of-senior-entrepreneurship.

Summer, Donna and Michael Omartian. *She Works Hard for the Money.* Chicago: Mercury Records, 1983.

Swedroe, Larry. "Why you should ignore economic forecasts." *CBS MoneyWatch,* November 26, 2012. http://www.cbsnews.com/news/why-you-should-ignore-economic-forecasts/

Thornberg Investment Management. "Cultivating the Growth of the Dividend." July 13, 2015. https://www.thornburg.com/pdf/TH1731_DividendStory.pdf

Van Knapp, David. "Has Dividend Growth Kept Up with Inflation?" *Seeking Alpha,* March 16, 2012. http://seekingalpha.com/article/439171-has-dividend-growth-kept-up-with-inflation.

Vernon, Steve. "Working in retirement is becoming the new normal." *CBS MoneyWatch,* June 12, 2014. http://www.cbsnews.com/news/working-in-retirement-is-becoming-the-new-normal/.

Wallace, Nick. "The Average Retirement Age in Every State in 2015." *Smartasset.com,* October 19, 2016. https://smartasset.com/retirement/average-retirement-age-in-every-state.

Ware, Bronnie. 2009. "Regrets of the Dying." *Inspiration and Chai,* November 19. http://bronnieware.com/regrets-of-the-dying/

Zero Dark Thirty. Directed by Kathryn Bigelow. 2012. Culver City: Sony Pictures Home Entertainment, 2013. Blu-ray.

Morgan James
Speakers Group

www.TheMorganJamesSpeakersGroup.com

We connect Morgan James published
authors with live and online events
and audiences who will benefit
from their expertise.

Morgan James makes all of our titles available
through the Library for All Charity Organization.

www.LibraryForAll.org

Printed in the USA
CPSIA information can be obtained
at www.ICGtesting.com
JSHW022221140824
68134JS00018B/1192

9 781683 505730